All of you who loved *The Girls with the Grandmother Faces, Midlife Musings* and *Speaking of the Girls* will recognize Frances Weaver's unique brand of humor and common sense in *This Year I Plan to Go Elsewhere.* Written for the woman who—after years of focusing on husband, children and work inside or outside the home— finds herself with financial independence, time on her hands and the urge to travel, *This Year I Plan to Go Elsewhere* offers a wealth of sound practical advice.

Frances draws on her own broad personal experience to offer tips for keeping things simple and traveling economically, planning a pleasant motor trip or picking the right ocean cruise. She explains how to find—and keep—congenial travel companions, handle money and be a self-starting adventurer. Best of all, she inspires you to get up and GO, whether it is for a day trip to a local point of interest, a week visiting the grandchildren or a grand tour around the world.

Last year I went around the world...
THIS YEAR I PLAN TO GO
ELSEWHERE

FRANCES WEAVER

drawings from the author's sketchbook

Fulcrum, Inc.
Golden, Colorado

Book Design by
Jody Chapel, Cover to Cover Design

Cover Illustration by
Patty Miller

Library of Congress Cataloging-in-Publication Data

Weaver, Frances
        1. Travel.   I. Title.

G151.W4 1989 910.4—dc19   88-31458
ISBN 1-55591-032-7

Printed in the United States
2   3   4   5   6   7   8   9   0

Fulcrum, Inc.
Golden, Colorado

CONTENTS

Introduction

Emily Katzenback astonishes me sometimes. We'll be riding along in a car, talking about nothing in particular and she'll come up with a remark like, "Oh, that's the way so many rooflines are in Belgium." And she's right. I know, because I've been there. Since widowhood rearranged my life eight years ago, I've been lots of places and have seen all sorts of rooflines.

"When were you in Belgium?" I'll say.

"Well, I haven't been there yet, but I've read a lot—especially about Brussels and Bruges. I enjoy that sort of thing. Keeps me thinking. I might never get to those places, but if I do, I'll know what to expect."

1

Emily is some kind of a traveler. She's been all over the world without leaving home. Emily can describe Taos Pueblo in New Mexico or South Street Seaport in New York City. She knows about the beauty of the Adirondack Park and the white-water rafting in Idaho or in Arkansas. Emily's secret is simple: Emily is aware. Around her hometown Emily knows every battlefield, every historic marker, every type of architecture. The "screen" in her mind must resemble an ever-changing Monet or Wyeth landscape.

On the other end of the stick is George Adams. George is the man who stood behind me on the deck of the *Royal Viking Sky* looking down at the Miraflores Lock of the Panama Canal and bellowed, "We came all the way down here just to see this? No wonder Jimmy Carter gave it back. These guys should take a good look at Hoover Dam if they want to see some real engineering."

Poor George has been to more ports and islands and far-away places with strange sounding names than most of the people I know, but he's never really left home. All he cares about is his own neighborhood. Wearing blinders as if he were running in the mud at Pimlico, with ear plugs in place to protect his preconceptions and prejudices, George travels because he can afford to and because it gives him something else to be an authority about—to complain about.

George is the same dreary guy who announces to his cronies at Rotary, "Don't go to France. You won't like it. Too many foreigners." Or, "Don't talk to me about your precious Indians. We saw some down in New Mexico living in mud houses. Geez, what a bunch!" George and his wife went to China when going to China was the posh thing to do. They took along jars of peanut butter. They'd tried Chinese food in San Francisco once and it was terrible, they said.

Somewhere in between Emily and George are the rest of us—you and I. We travel for different reasons, choose from hundreds of types of vacations. It's *our* travel which is the purpose of this book. Sharing ideas and experiences is only part of our traveling world, our mobile society. All we need is time to tie our sneakers.

SENSE of DIRECTION

We gotta be goin'
Where're we goin'
What're we gonna do?

Right along the tracks, keeping time with Amtrak clacking, those words rattled inside my head across Illinois, Iowa, Missouri, Kansas. I was traveling the same trail taken by the forefathers of this Weaver family when they moved to north central Kansas from Iowa more than 100 years ago. Only they walked. Those people drove sheep ahead of them, carried all of their worldly possessions and walked all the way to Kansas.

From the windows of my train, the fields and farms stretched to infinity. What a trip for a bunch of farmers. Grandpa Cool was an old man before I met him, but Grandpa Cool never forgot

3

or failed to mention the longest walk of his life. He never really recovered from it, although he was just a kid at the time, back in the 1870s. And after walking hundreds of miles behind several hundred sheep, he never touched a bite of lamb again as long as he lived. As far as I know, he never went any farther from the home place than the cattle market in Kansas City either. One cross-country journey was enough for Grandpa.

Whether walking, riding, flying, floating, hitchhiking or going over Niagara Falls in a barrel or racing on the Salt Flats, we all have travel experiences. Most of us are adding to our travel diaries regularly, particularly those of us who have outgrown the demands of a growing family or outlasted the restrictions of a younger lifestyle. We're the mobile generation.

Picking up a huge collection of snapshots from the developers after an extended stay in Greece and other exotic places, I was tickled by the attitude of the girl behind the counter. She was a classmate of mine at Adirondack Community College, but she was college age. "I wish I could travel to all these exciting countries like you and Professor Rikhoff," she whined.

"Oh, but you can," said I soothingly, "as soon as you get to be my age."

"Ye gods, I don't want to wait *that* long!"

She blushed, I smiled.

The title for this book says the same thing. I found it in a cartoon. An old lady at the counter of the travel agency is saying, "Last year I took a trip around the world. This year I plan to go elsewhere."

So where is elsewhere? As near or as far from home as we want it to be. And how will we get there? At this moment some bedeviled soul is out there trying to locate one more remote Caribbean island, one more Greek ruin, one more perfect topless beach, one more coral reef, one more unheard-of Hindu temple, or one more Treasure House of Britain to add to the itineraries of the world, to tempt one more would-be tourist out of an armchair into a deck chair.

Travel is big, big business. Conversely, business is a lot of travel. However, we are concerned here with tourism travel, recreational travel, which seems to flourish no matter what rocks the stock market or threatens the dollar.

Recreational travel is, in a sense, atavistic. What mankind used to do for survival has become, over the ages, a leisure activity—like hunting or baking your own bread. Those ancient nomads seeking the next oasis for water were kindred spirits with the '49ers searching for one big strike at Sutter's Mill. We have always moved on to better our lives in one way or another. Look at Queen Isabella or Marco Polo or Brigham Young. Today we continue to move all over the world, still improving our lives, but in a more subtle fashion.

Widening horizons—that's what it's about. We have more opportunities to know and understand more about the world we live in than any generation; even I, for one, have a lot to learn. I still can't figure out how anyone could have made maps or charted shipping lanes across the seas without being able to look at the whole world from a satellite.

Regina Porter, lifelong New Yorker, visited me in Colorado two years ago. This was one of those magical weeks in February when Colorado forgot about winter. Shirt-sleeve weather. The sun shone, the wind hid in the high mountains, the sky was the clearest of bright blue, unknown to most of the world. One morning, Regina stood staring and gazing at Pikes Peak against that almost-too-blue-to-be-true background and said, "Where are the clouds?"

"There aren't any today," I replied matter of factly.

Regina just stood there. "All my life I've heard songs and poems about 'the skies are not cloudy all day,' and I thought somebody made that up," she said. Since that Colorado visit Regina's horizons have broadened. More of the world is real to her than before. Being there made the difference. Being there made the difference a year later too, when she went to the desert (in Arizona) for the first time—cactus, lizards, cloud-bursts—all real.

The "being there" experience has brought new understandings to most of us. For example, Miss Sarah, youngest grandchild in our clan, spent four days in New York City with me. Her cousin Kacie came with us. These girls were 11 and 12 years old. We put in four nonstop days from Bloomingdale's to the Metropolitan Museum, from a Broadway show to a Circle Line cruise. For the rest of their lives, these youngsters will not see a rerun of Barney Miller without recognizing the Empire State building in the opening shots. But it's more than that. They will forever have a sense of the feeling of the city. One glimpse of the skyline will bring back the glamour of the Waldorf-Astoria, the pretzels and kebobs from the street vendors, the majesty of the Statue of Liberty, the plight of an AIDS victim begging on the corner or of a bag lady clawing through trash for pop cans. They will hear the noises, breathe in the smells, see the taxis, feel the city. No amount of reading, TV viewing or second-hand descriptions could do that. The more those kids see of the world, the more they will understand the way it works.

These same sensations, these aftertastes of travel experiences, are just as important at any age, of course. New York was asphalt and pollution to me until my first writer's conference at Saratoga Springs. *That* New York actually looked like those Hudson River School paintings. Along Lake George I watched for the last of the Mohicans and found out that the French and Indian War was more than the three-page skirmish found in seventh-grade history books.

Our reading, our conversation, our everyday appreciation grows with every travel experience. Even the most lavish books on archaeology or prehistoric beginnings cannot bring us close to the wonder we feel standing before pictographs on the walls of a cave dwelling in New Mexico. Bending over to scratch in the dry dust of Mesa Verde—and discovering that the rock you just kicked is actually a fragment of pottery perhaps a thousand years old—turns a casual vacation into a memorable hands-on learning experience at any age.

Side trips to watch glassblowers blowing, potters potting, carvers uncovering life-like figures from a dead stick add to our awareness. Excursions to copper mines, burial grounds, local museums, stagecoach stops and battlegrounds—the list of life-expanding opportunities around us is endless.

These days it's not necessary to take a slow boat to China or spend money we ought to leave for the grandchildren to stretch our own vision beyond boredom. We can learn a lot, enjoy so much, and appreciate ourselves and our surroundings with simplified, well-planned, self-starting travel tailored for our own lives. That's not hard to do. Meeting the challenge of planning becomes the goal.

Look at these synonyms for "trip": journey, tour, excursion, outing, junket, commute, trek, expedition, voyage, cruise, pilgrimage, hike and folly.

That word "trip" can also mean: stumble, sprawl, blunder, ramble, miscalculation, schlep or dance (the light fantastic?), frolic, leap, frisk, and muff, flub, louse-up or blow it.

You decide which of those words best fit the kind of travel you'd enjoy, then let's get going. At least we won't have to trudge along behind a flock of sheep.

What Are We Going to Do?

Kathy Frantz and her parents rank as specialized travelers in my opinion. They appreciate and make a study of covered bridges. That's right. Covered bridges. They travel all around the Northeast from their home in Saratoga Springs, targeting one bridge or several. Then they make a field trip with other covered-bridge enthusiasts or on their own.

Bridges, especially covered bridges, don't exist in a vacuum. Surrounded by the history and the people who settled a locality, bridges literally opened worlds to these folks. Who built them? Who crossed them? Now that covered bridges appear on the endangered lists, these bridge fans find themselves involved in preservation, marking historic crossings.

Kathy's telling me about bridges reminds me of the trip I intend to take one of these days. I want to cross upstate New York along I-90 just to look at the old barns. I've noticed magnificent barns along there. And I've spotted special limestone fence posts I want to inspect, but that will have to be another trip.

Fran and Jim Hensen are making their plans to get to the gem show in Tucson this year. They've checked out gem shows in different parts of the country, particularly in the Southwest. Tucson has one of the best, they say. Besides, the drive to Tucson from Colorado is always interesting, with such a variety of side jaunts (to the mines at Morenci or the ruins at Tuzigoot, maybe) to make this more of an adventure than fleeing to Arizona just because Colorado winters are colder.

Jim retired from anesthesiology. "We're goin' someplace or planning a trip most of the time now," Fran says. "When Jim first retired, we thought we'd move up to Colorado Springs to be closer to our kids and their families, but then we said, 'They don't need us in their back pockets or lookin' over their shoulders every day'. So we're stayin' here in our own house and doin' what we've always wanted to do. We heard about another gem show that's out in the desert with the people all in trailers, right near some of the turquoise mines and all that. Wouldn't that be great?"

And how about the train buffs? Some of them get even more excited than rock hounds. Narrow gauge or regular tracks, trains attract more admirers just for the joy of the ride than any other form of transportation except cruise ships, perhaps.

When our son, Matt, was about 12, my husband, John, and I decided to try the much-celebrated run from Antonito, Colorado, to Chama, New Mexico. The Cumbres and Toltec Railroad over Cumbres Pass was newly restored and operating with steam engines and everything. Passengers often had to help put out brush fires started by flying sparks along the high-mountain route. Sounded like fun.

The first thing we noticed about our fellow travelers was the way they dressed. Some were wearing regulation brakeman's coveralls. Some wore railroader's caps with a variety of emblems, like "Chesapeake and Ohio" or "Santa Fe." Others sported jackets adorned with patches from railroads all over the world. "We're in a hotbed of train nuts," John said. We soon realized how right he was. Their dedication was masterful. Since we couldn't engage them in conversation about the sorts and conditions of oil cans used by assorted railroads for specific purposes, the amateur Weaver family didn't count much on that train.

The best part turned out to be the photographers' ritual. Those shutterbugs weren't even *on* the train.

During that four-hour journey, the tracks intersected with the highway across Cumbres Pass several times. "Look how many cars are stopped for the train, Mom. I didn't think there was much traffic up here in the mountains." Matt was right. As many as 30 cars were parked, waiting for the train to pass. At the next crossing, we noticed the same thing—parked cars. But there were no people in the cars. Scattered up and down along the railroad track we saw flocks of men, women and kids dressed in trainman garb, armed with tripods and fancy cameras. As we rode by, we shouted and waved. They took pictures of us and our train. Eventually, we took pictures of them too.

There might be more than a dozen of those crossings. Each time we ran into the highway, those camera/train bugs were there; same cars, same people, same train to take a picture of. At the trestles, they nearly lost their minds with the glory of it all. At the end of the line that crowd disappeared as quickly as it had materialized. Off to the darkroom, I suppose.

These are simple examples of travel for a purpose. You can suggest dozens more with a little thought. Paul Stone has toured large sections of the country by bus, searching out houses and buildings designed by Frank Lloyd Wright. Elizabeth Pomada and Michael Larson became so intrigued by Victorian architecture, they've written and illustrated two books to guide the rest of us to such treasures of early America.

Bird watchers, backpackers, bikers have specific purposes in traveling. So do scuba divers and hot-air balloonists. Or collectors of antique bottles or Burma Shave signs. Everyone we know can find some reason to explore or discover new haunts.

Why is this subject of such import that it ranks as the second chapter of this book? Because of some of the negative examples we see every day.

"This is a terrible cruise. Dull. I hate the Caribbean, anyway. But where else is there to go this time of year?"

"We had a lousy time. All George wanted to do was play golf, of course, and it rained four days while we were trapped in our hotel room. Hundreds of dollars just for that!"

"There's not much to shop for here. Besides, all the stores have the same stuff and we can get most of it cheaper at K-Mart at home."

"Well, Betty and the children had a good time, I suppose, out on the beach all day getting terrible sunburns and picking up silly little shells. I just sat in my room, out of that dreadful sun. I hate sand on my feet and sitting on a wrinkled old towel and all that."

"Margaret kept telling me I was having a good time, but I say if you've seen one castle, you've seen 'em all. And we saw them all last year in Germany and the year before in Ireland."

Cure for these woes of the misbegotten vacation? Simple. Only one question is important: "Why should we go there?" If the answer is, "One of the girls at the office said it would be fun," or, "This dreary winter weather is driving me mad," or, "There's nothing to do here at home," give the matter more thought. If you are bored at home, it's a safe bet you'll be bored someplace else, unless you have a real purpose in being there. It's no more stimulating to sit around in Scottsdale than it is in St. Paul in February if you haven't an agenda—a plan of action longer than a list of restaurants.

Think about these things:

What will we do if it rains?

How much can we learn there?

What should I read before we leave home?

Is this place just like home, only warmer? Or cooler?

Exactly what is the focus of this trip?

Then find out about:

Mexican cookery classes in Taos, New Mexico.

Homestays abroad for seniors.

Barge trips on the Champlain Canal of the Hudson River.

Smithsonian study groups here and abroad.

The small museums within 400 miles of your front door.

The ferry system of Washington State.

Elderhostel. There's so much to learn about Elderhostel. (See Chapter 4 for just one example.)

Participatory research with Earth Watch or the Oceanic Society.

Some travel goals require more than one trip, of course. My fascination with cheeseburgers has turned into a continuing quest wherever I go. I'm beginning a concentrated effort to find a hamburger joint exactly like the ones described in my new favorite book, *Roadside Food*, a colorful paperback written by LeRoy Woodson and some of his friends. The subtitle is *Good Home-Style Cooking across America*. Now any number of eggheads from coast to coast thrive on research, but I'll bet none has thrived better than this Woodson gang on their project. This is not specifically a guide listing the ten best burger heavens in the state of Tennessee. Instead, various types of traditional everyday fare are discussed in terms of perfection.

Mouth-watering pictures brought me to the realization that these days of exotic pasta creations, sun-dried tomatoes, smoked duck salads and wild mushroom caviar are stimulating in their own way, but a freshly cooked real-life hamburger? Unbeatable!

Ralph Gardner, Jr., is the writer of the burger chapter. This man is such an artist with words, I'm sitting here at the word processor salivating as I review his text: "The cheeseburger sings the praises of our republic more melodiously than any anthem. . . . Only in America is deluxe defined as a thimble-size cup of cole slaw, a lettuce leaf with three slices of tomato, and a side of fries."

The expertise of a good short-order cook in a first-class diner seems to inspire nothing less than awe in the eyes of these aficionados of the sizzling grill, the bun soft as a baby's bottom, and the "cheese which melts and runs down the side of the burger like lava down the slopes of Vesuvius." A good grill cook

12

apparently knows exactly when each burger on the grill is ready for the flip and for the cheese.

In this quest for the perfect burger diner, the fast-food chains don't count. This is understandable. The greatest joy of this sort of burger dining is individual preparation of *your* burger. Says our man Gardner, "There's something sinister and totalitarian about a bushel of styrofoam-encapsulated Big Macs sitting under a heat lamp . . . orders filled before they were even placed." The customer needs a sense of belonging—wants to be a sidelines participant in the creation of such a wonder as is pictured on the back cover of the book.

Certainly the proper preparation of fries is discussed. The choice of condiments is left to our discretion. "If you want to dump a relish that looks and tastes like Chiclets on your burger, that's your business."

That finest expression of the art of burger-consumption—coming out even with the burger, fries and pickle at the last bite—tops off this gourmet reading experience. So be it.

Now where can I find such a pleasure palace? I'll keep looking. That gives me an added target, no matter where I go.

There are all sorts of purposes for travel to consider, including collecting posters and postcards from major and small art collections; touring battlefields, courthouses and nature preserves; going white-water rafting; picking your own produce; following the Spanish Mission Trail or the Natchez Trace—all intended to widen our own horizons and to share in an ever-growing circle of friends.

Ready? All you need is an open mind and a big map.

One Wayfaring Stranger

"Alone? All by yourself? You won't know a single person on that whole ship? For a month? Alone?"

Martha's look, her tone of voice, said, "You've gotta be crazy."

What she actually said was, "Boy, are you brave!"

That was back in 1981. I was ready to travel, to test my ability to get places on my own. But traveling alone had not been my style so far. I had grown up, as most of us have, traveling with family or friends. Until my first writers' conference in Santa Barbara in my early fifties, I had never ventured forth on my own any farther than the hundred miles to Denver for meetings of the Colonial Dames.

We live in a Noah's Ark world. Boarding the ship, walking alone up the gangplank, that immutable fact hit me like a ton of bricks. I had the weird sensation of being followed by two giraffes and a pair of monkeys. Since walking two-by-two with the rest of the first graders to the gym, almost every aspect of our lives is paired-up. And there I was, alone. Uneasy? I suppose so. Scared? Looking back, I'm not certain. But there was no turning back at that point. Let's look with some detail at that first lone-traveler experience, which was no different for me than for anyone else in like circumstances.

While being ushered to my stateroom, I looked around enough to satisfy initial curiosity. This was my first Royal Viking cruise. I had been on other ships, but not many. And not alone.

Out on the decks the ship's orchestra was playing, champagne was being served, and everyone seemed to have a year's supply of those maddening curly streamers to toss over the rail. F. Scott Fitzgerald would have loved the scene. I declined the champagne, but accepted a roll of streamers from a uniformed person—and the fun began. No way could I get *my* streamers to uncoil gracefully and drift toward the crowds on the pier. Merrymakers around me were shouting, dancing, singing. I smiled at the woman next to me at the rail.

"I can't make these blasted things unroll," she said. I had found my first friend.

First night out at dinner was slow, to say the least. I had asked for seating at a table for eight. Six of us appeared, but not the cruise director, who was to be the ship's host at our table. Three of us sat almost totally silent while three loudmouths from Connecticut bragged to each other about everything from their stock holdings to their four-car garages and the number of Royal Viking cruises they had taken before. At that point I had second thoughts about my Great Adventure.

Immediately after dinner I wandered into the main lounge, determined to make this work. There sat two lovely looking ladies—relaxed, smiling. "Are you dance watchers too?" I asked. They said, "Sit with us." That's how I met Skippy and Marion, the beginning of a warm, lasting friendship. In those two weeks we laughed, joked, exchanged old stories and shared new experiences, building an invaluable association for the rest of our lives.

That first real step made the rest of the trip a delight. Four couples traveling together invited me to join them for cocktails "anytime." Other single women were good companions on shore excursions.

On board ship there are limitless opportunities for striking up conversations. Every morning puzzle sheets are available for passengers to fuss over until bingo time. Comparing answers and hints about these omnipresent word-games becomes the key to meeting fellow travelers. So do the other activities, from morning exercise classes to the midnight buffet. I appreciated the relaxed atmosphere and the casual conversations. Dinner-table talk improved too, once we all got past the rite of establishing the importance of living in Connecticut. On the last day at sea, I had a lunchtime party for my new friends, passengers and ship's staff. Fine.

Even a cruise can offer more than the expected eating and entertainment. Establishing your own purpose in the way you spend leisure time is not only plausible, but highly recommended on cruise ships. That's why there are so many varied activities on board. Nobody on the staff expects each passenger to become an expert at needlepoint or backgammon or golf or calligraphy. Those lessons are offered so that people make contact with other passengers who enjoy the same thing. Once you've been to one bridge lecture, other bridge players will recognize you as "one of us."

The prospect of trying to meet and get along with the entire passenger list would scare even the most extraverted among us. Consider the cruise experience an opportunity to see a new part of the world and to meet some kindred spirits in the casino, lounging beside the pool or jogging on the deck. That attractive person at the next table probably feels as much at sea as you on that first night out. Once you've met through a shared interest, there you are; you have a new friend, so you're not alone anymore.

"I'd have a dreadful time traveling on my own. I can't remember *anyone's* name." Most of us share that problem. What to do? Show enough interest in new acquaintances to ask them to repeat their names. That's a courtesy that we can all appreciate. Then repeat your own name in the course of conversation. Inviting a new-found friend to share a cab in the next port is difficult unless you know the name. Sometimes a memory-jogging gimmick works. For example, I once told a tale about a butcher who wrote "Weaver" on all of the packages of meat sent to our house—instead of "pork chops" or "ground beef" as I had requested. This story is a favorite of mine, and reinforces my name with new people. I quit using the anecdote, however, when a bright young woman introduced me to her tablemates as "Frances Butcher."

One never-fail rule for meeting people? Ask questions. Even if you don't particularly care about the answers, ask anyway. Expressing interest in the other person is as important while traveling alone as it is in the rest of our daily lives. You might meet some dull folks, but you'll also meet worthwhile new companions—and expanding your horizons is what travel is all about.

Striking out on your own makes much more sense, for men or women, if you choose purpose-oriented traveling. One example from my own observation is the archaeological dig at Crow Canyon in Colorado. In this case, I was accompanied by family, but I enjoyed watching the singles. Forty or more people participated in that week-long adventure into the remains of Anasazi culture in the Southwest, older singles who had no intention of starting a career in that field. They simply wanted to take part in one dig. From the moment of arrival, those men and women were surrounded by others of similar age and interest who had something to talk about. Through the week they established close friendships because of their common concern about what had become of the forefathers of the Pueblo and Navajo tribes. Conversations at the dining table, in the laboratory or out in the digging sites were easy, uncomplicated, not self-conscious. Attending writers' conferences is another example of discovering a mutual interest with other single travelers. Actually, going alone on a trip of this sort is a much better way to meet new friends and find new outlets than having a "partner" along.

Traveling on our own involves much more than finding someone to talk to, naturally. Being able to make and trust our own decisions is most important. Other concerns have to do with money management, luggage, dining alone and making the most of entertainment and sightseeing options.

Making and trusting our own decisions counts even more away from home, away from the people we depend upon for confirmation of our own judgment. Deciding on accommodations, transportation, final destinations and the like has been done before the travel begins, but details about side trips and such seem to paralyze some people. Attitude becomes even more important. "I'd best take a cab," or "I'd rather walk," or "Beach today, shop tomorrow"; what weight oil to put in the car or amount of air pressure for the tires, which route will be most scenic, which most practical? Myriad choices must be made. Trust yourself and, best of all, keep asking, "Is this a life-threatening situation?" Then relax, decide what seems best to you, and enjoy the rest of the adventure.

That old bugaboo, money management, looms large when traveling alone. Keep in mind that there will be nobody at hand when you want to ask, "Do you have an extra quarter for the tip?" or "Do you have any ones?" when the taxi driver refuses to take a twenty-dollar bill for a three-dollar fare. Just as surely as you check to be certain you have a lipstick, room key, identification and Kleenex, check the denominations of the money you're carrying. And try not to run out of money. Even in this day and age of money-spewing machines in every airport and major lobby, being short of cash can be a trial. And an embarrassment. It can make any of us feel very much alone.

Credit cards, particularly Visa, are acceptable almost any place around the world today. I was astonished when I asked for cash in the Peace Hotel in Shanghai in 1981 and showed the clerk my Mastercard. All she said was, "How much money do you want?" I replied, "Well, how much do you have?" But there surely was no trouble, at least not until I was back home trying to pay the bill. Since that time, credit cards have become even more acceptable.

Handling luggage can be a big problem or not, depending on how smart we are in our packing in the first place. If you're the only one to carry the luggage, then taking extra shoes and matching purses for each outfit plus different coats for rain or sunshine becomes foolish, doesn't it? Whether we are pushing and shoving our own bags into the trunk of a car, onto Amtrak or into the overhead compartment in an overcrowded plane, we look, feel and cope better with the least possible load. Practice at home with your various carry-ons, hanger cases and larger luggage. If you can't hoist that sucker onto your own closet shelf, how are you going to be your calm, cool sophisticated self in the aisle of a 727? Pack whatever mixes and matches. Take minimum underwear. Leave the wrinkle-prone stuff at home.

Eating alone sometimes means room service. At first, I resorted to a club sandwich in the room very often, but there's something taste-destroying about the elevator distance from the kitchen to a hotel room. Everything on the tray turns to cardboard. Soggy cardboard at that. So eat in the hotel restaurant or someplace nearby when traveling alone. But eat early. There's a better choice of tables, and the service is usually faster. I've found it's best to call for a reservation at any hour and to be frank about the situation. "Look, I'm dining alone tonight and I'd rather not have a table stuck out in the middle of the room or behind the kitchen door. A quiet corner will be nice." If you're intending to dine in a superspecial place, ask if unescorted ladies are comfortable in this restaurant. Hotel restaurants are used to single women. It may be best to save the mind-expanding gourmet thrills for sometime when you have a companion.

Breakfast and lunch pose no problem in eating alone for me. I've even gotten past taking something along to read or write. Just sit there, relax, look around, eavesdrop and make up little stories about the other folks in the café. You'll be fine.

Entertainment? When planning one-person travel, it's smart to read local papers from the area you're headed for ahead of time. That way you'll know whether or not an ice show or a rodeo or a quilt display or a particularly wonderful exhibition of contemporary art is in the city. In the country, there might be bluegrass festivals or readings by local poets and writers. In the absence of newspapers, information from chambers of commerce, local colleges and libraries will serve the purpose.

At your destination, the magazines in motel and hotel rooms provide excellent suggestions for entertainment. In Tucson, my friend Regina and I were entranced by an Arizona Theater production of *On the Verge*, a wonderful play that we would have missed if the room copy of local events had not alerted us. One person can almost always get a theater ticket. Just be certain you can find your way back to the hotel. (I am assuming my readers are alert enough to ask about the safety of venturing out on the streets alone and after dark. Security is an ever-growing concern. Sometimes it's best to settle for a matinée.)

Sightseeing? In a strange city, nothing beats a Grayline tour for an overall idea of the important and interesting local attractions. You can handle this by yourself anywhere. Information is in almost any hotel lobby or phone directory. Once you have a Grayline overview, you will know what buildings, parks, monuments and so forth to take a closer look at on your own. As one person, hiring a car and driver just to see the beaches and a stadium is expensive and dull.

The same holds true for harbor cruises as for Grayline tours: Don't fret if this is "touristy." The other tourists won't mind having you along. Alone.

What are the benefits of traveling solo?
1. You meet more people in group situations, such as cruises, group tours and such.
2. Rooming alone is more comfortable than sharing closets and the counter space in the bathroom.
3. Your time schedule is your own—not tied to waiting for someone else or keeping anyone else waiting.
4. Choices of food and beverage are your own, not dependent on a roommate's allergies or digestive peculiarities.

5. In case of necessary change of plans, you won't waste half a day saying, "Well, I don't care. What do *you* want to do?"

Not every trip should be a solitary experience, but once in a while it's good for all of us. Give it a try.

Safety in Numbers

Yes, we do live in a Noah's Ark world. No doubt about that. In this chapter we'll begin by exploring travel two-by-two, then share a few of the innumerable opportunities for group travel that are gaining popularity.

Travel and Leisure, the American Express magazine renowned and trusted as one of the world's most reliable travel-guide periodicals, has been known to devote entire issues to travel by two's. "Isn't it romantic?" they say. Romantic, it surely is. Being alone together can't be beat—in the right situation. Some travel spots are absolutely made for this sort of experience.

Glamor capitals like Venice, Paris, Vienna qualify for *Travel and Leisure*'s choices of vacations for two. The South Pacific is high on the list of romantic watering holes too. Well, that's just fine for the small percentage of lovers who can afford that sort of dream. They don't need to buy books like this one to tell them where to go. Let's get to the more affordable and practical places closer at hand but still ideal for twosome travel.

"There's a Small Hotel" ought to be the theme song for this subject. Actually, that song refers to an inn in Santa Barbara that is still a fine retreat for two. There are any number of places to go around Santa Barbara—the beaches, the mission, the nearby countryside, artists' galleries and museums—all low-key excitement.

Most of the California coastline is scenic, but I certainly would find it hard to maintain a romantic spirit tied up in a traffic jam for two hours on the L.A. freeway. So here's suggestion number one: avoid congested areas.

Two persons in a car too long can easily become a crowd. One time, a gentleman friend from Connecticut offered to drive me to upstate New York. Bless his heart, he was of the "old school." There was no question of his intentions. He would drive me to Glens Falls, period. Leaving his house, I said, "You know, we could pretend we're married on this trip if you want to." He looked like he might faint until I explained the remark, "You drive, I'll hold the map and we'll fight about it."

Too often, that's the married way to travel. Which brings up suggestion number two: Agree about how to get wherever you're going before leaving home. Be specific. Vague doesn't count.

Here are some scenic regions in the United States that I recommend as vacation destinations for two people—couples or not. To avoid congestion, I'd start with upstate New York and Vermont. Or the Taos–Santa Fe area. Chesapeake Bay holds a fascination with its small towns and picturesque villages not too far from urban centers. The hills of Arkansas appeal to most independent travelers. Other interesting areas are Carefree or Sedona in Arizona, the Outer Banks of North Carolina and the Pennsylvania Dutch Country. Covering this land are attractive, accessible touring spots, all waiting to be explored. You can name a dozen more, I'm sure.

Vacations for two differ little from other travel—first of all, you need a mutually agreed upon purpose. My friend Jean Rikhoff and I agreed, before we took off on an extended summer's journey through Greece, Italy and France, that we were literally tracing or following the spread of civilization from the ancient Greeks through Roman days to modern France. Each stop meant another museum or archaeological dig. We also agreed ahead of time to spend about half of our time on beaches. We both knew those ground rules and the trip worked just fine.

What did not work in our day-to-day driving tour were two unexpected areas of discomfort: the excess stuff we both dragged along and too many hours in a car without outside contacts.

By the end of two months we were tired of our heavy luggage, tired of our clothes and tired of our own company. I'm happy to report the friendship was strong enough to withstand the pressure of too much togetherness, but it was a struggle. Remedy? We should have given up roadside picnic lunches and joined a crowded eatery for one thing. We should have hung out in more bars, just to have somebody else to talk to.

I figured out Rick had about had it with me one day when she stopped suddenly right in front of me on one of those narrow sidewalks made of rough stones. We were being sideswiped by speeding Fiats because we couldn't duck into doorways fast enough. "Okay!" shouted my English professor traveling companion, "We've had enough of quaint. Just bring out the regular sidewalks."

When two women decide to travel together, planning looms exceedingly important insofar as duplication of gadgets is concerned. There should be only one hair dryer, one laundry "line," one flashlight, maybe even only one guide book. Otherwise, the room overflows with equipment and reading material before the first bag is unzipped. With careful planning, your trip for two can be a big success.

Slightly larger groups? Three or four on a day trip is ideal, although four is better than three, since nobody really enjoys riding in the back seat alone or being the "odd person" in any situation. You may be interested in a longer trip, however, should travel with a few friends be a radical concept for you, start small. Round up three passengers for an overnight trip no more than 150 miles from home. Most of us grow old immersed in the belief that staying all night less than four hours away from home is an unacceptable self-indulgence. Now we know better.

Not far from you is an art museum, a theater, a lecture series or a marvelous concert. Go. Spend the night. Making hotel reservations is easy in this day of hotel and motel chains, most of which have an 800 number. Take only what you will need. Check the size of the trunk before you decide whose car to take. Split up the driving time if the distance is great. (Chapter 6 covers these arrangements and many others involving travel by car.)

Another idea for a small group excursion: Three or four of you join in a larger, amorphous group, but remain a "core" within it. For example, I've known women whose "bridge group" travels together on cruises, on Amtrak journeys (playing bridge from Chicago to Albany should be about right) or on museum tours. (Of course, you can join a group program as an individual as well as with family or friends.)

Choices multiply almost daily for group travel. Going someplace with a preplanned group tour offers many advantages, such as group rates in hotels, on planes and so on. (Often individuals cannot get reservations at peak season in popular resort areas because groups have booked all available space.) Luggage handling and transfers from airports or train stations to hotels are taken care of by the organizer of the tour. Often, your all-inclusive fare includes many meals and tipping, so messing with money is minimal.

All sorts and conditions of group travel can be found on the market these days. Consult your favorite travel agent, to begin the process. Some tours are "guided," some are "escorted." TWA has a dandy series called "Getaway Vacations," which offers the best options I know of. Luggage handling, reservations, transfers and such are all provided, but guided sightseeing tours are optional. This leaves you free of the worries of nitty-gritty details, while you may choose to wander around on your own or with the crowd. Just be certain your luggage is outside your door when it's time to move along.

Discount travel operators in many localities sell group tripping solely for the purpose of sightseeing and shopping, hitting the high spots at every stop. These are often the "This is Tuesday, must be Belgium," sort of travel vendors. Usually their prices are lower than other travel plans because you get less—very little personal attention or service. I'd say ask a lot of questions to avoid surprises and disappointments.

AAA (American Automobile Association) claims to be the largest travel agency in this country, maybe the world. Booking group travel through AAA can be well worthwhile, since they can offer much lower fares on some cruises and tours but do not treat clients like inmates or happy campers.

AARP (American Association of Retired Persons) is another purveyor of group travel that has expanded by leaps and bounds in the past few years. Offerings include American vacations, cruises and longer stays abroad. Passengers can be assured of travel companions of like age and relatively similar tastes in music, food and sleeping accommodations. They might have a curfew, which I think means nobody has to stay up past ten.

Winter holiday travel with family or in tour groups seems to be more popular than ever. For some of us at holiday time, being in a fascinating faraway place, or in the midst of one of the fabled cities of Europe, beats whatever is at home. Linblad Travel offers a Scandinavian Christmas, which includes Christmas Eve before a roaring fire in the Siljanshill Hotel in Rattvik, complete with tree trimming, and a traditional smorgasbord, sleigh rides, all sorts of wonderful celebrating. Or you might prefer a Victorian Holiday at the King's Head Hotel in Cotswolds, where Christmas merrymaking is as lively as in Sweden. The King's Head is a Best Western hotel. Olson's Europe offers a 14-day package of the same sort in Switzerland and Austria.

On our side of the world, Maupintour plans an eight-day Christmas in the Southwest, including Christmas Eve in Santa

Fe, where the luminarias lighting those angular buildings prompt a delightful frisson, leaving a memory that most find unforgettable. In New England, Christmas holiday tours and package deals abound. The Orchards in Williamstown, Massachusetts, is a fine example. Add to these the ski vacations for families and the special cruises to warmer climes, and your Christmas can be special almost anyplace.

One thought I like: giving my family a Christmas vacation instead of a bunch of sweaters that don't fit. It's a fine way to share Christmas fun. This is particularly true if we plan together, and choose a place where it's convenient to "break up into smaller groups." Do *not* "favor" your family with a Disney World type of vacation at holiday time—too crowded to be any fun for the kids or their parents and most of all, for their grandparents. Incidentally, we work out finances carefully before finalizing the trip. I can't foot all the bills, but my gift to them is making the experience affordable for all of us.

Very interesting to me are the travel groups that add another dimension—learning—to going somewhere. On the inside back page of *Smithsonian* magazine you will find listings of countryside tours, foreign and domestic travel, coupled with lecture, museum and classroom experiences in places like Oxford; Tuscany; Washington, D.C.; China or Crow Canyon, Colorado. Plans made by the Smithsonian staff are strictly first cabin. The majestic *Sea Cloud* carries Smithsonian travelers through the Panama Canal or around the Mediterranean. Scholars accompany these groups. Learning is an integral part of the daily routine. Fellow travelers make good dinner conversationalists and excellent companions on field trips. Their curiosities are alive. They want to expand horizons, or they would not be there.

My own Smithsonian experiences represent a true sampling of the sort of travel available with them. First of all, I tried a writers' seminar in Washington, D.C., for a week. The course was conducted by Edwards Park, and this is how it worked. Participants were housed at a very special rate in the Capital Holiday Inn, which is just behind the Air and Space Museum.

Classes were held in a government office building across the street in a classroom setting with blackboards and all that. About 35 writers of varying experience and interest sat in a lecture situation, then worked on in-class and overnight assignments. I mean, we really worked. And we were expected to read our work. Edwards Park, who writes a monthly *Smithsonian* column, "Around the Mall and Beyond," taught us in the manner of his composition classes at Yale. We learned more about writing than I thought anyone could absorb in a week. From this first Smithsonian seminar I became a columnist.

Since 1979 the Smithsonian Institution has been bringing Americans to Worcester College, Oxford, one hundred or so at a time. Courses of study range from prehistoric Europe to the English country house. Answering the ad in the back of the *Smithsonian* magazine is the only qualification for admission to the seminar which is designed, according to Selected Studies Director Wilton Dillon, for those of us who strive to keep curiosity alive in ourselves.

Boarding PanAm 106 at Dulles airport, we didn't resemble any group of college students I've ever imagined. There were some young adults, but the average age was probably 55. Our uniform dress code was clearly in evidence: ladies wore tailored or knit suits, sensible shoes, short hairdos, and not too much makeup. The men appeared to be dressed for Rotary. No plaid pants or running shoes on our guys. Each one of us carried a raincoat. Everyone sporting the blue and yellow Smithsonian Associates badge wore something more, however: a look of expectancy. We were on our way to something special, and it showed.

A pretty young girl tapped my arm. "Who are these people?"

"College students," I told her. "We're the freshman class at Oxford. Forgot our beanies."

About that time one of our ladies decided she had lost her passport while trying to protect the film in her camera from the X-ray machine. Turned out to be freshman jitters; she found it in her pocket. Another classmate became nearly frantic hunting for her boarding pass. Two of her friends—same age, same height, as much alike as any schoolgirls anyplace—fished the elusive card from the depths of an overloaded nine-pound purse. We boarded two-by-two.

For two weeks we stayed in the dormitories, some new, some from the fifteenth century. We ate in the Great Hall, where pomp and ceremony marked the beginning of each evening meal. We had field trips to Blenheim Castle and Stratford. And we had one hilarious time. My course was "Oxfordshire." About twelve of us took copious notes through a lecture in the local museum, then spent the rest of the day in a van tripping around to inspect the places we'd been lectured about. We concentrated on places with names like "The Great Tithe Barn" or "Chipping Norton."

Right now you may feel free to ask me anything you've ever wanted to know about Chipping Norton or Witney or Burford in the middle of the English countryside. Perhaps you'd prefer information about Great Tew—which almost fell down. Just ask. I'm your girl, believe me. After a fortnight (I almost said, "two weeks") of intensive study about Oxfordshire, I returned to Lake George knowing more than I ever wanted to know about such places—probably more than anyone around here wants to know. I have been saturated with rural England from pre-Roman times to today and I enjoyed every minute of it.

Here again, the Smithsonian participants were interesting people to whom learning was important. From these experiences I have at least a dozen friends whom I see and correspond with regularly. Our lives were enormously expanded by that campus and that wonderfully historic place.

After a second session of magazine writing back at the home base, my next Smithsonian trip was entirely different but equally rewarding. This was the archaeological study I mentioned earlier. I had waited two years for my grandsons, Whit and Jason, to be 15 years old, so we could go to Crow Canyon in southwest Colorado for a Smithsonian dig. My daughter came with us, and we had the best time any four relatives traveling together could have anyplace.

At Crow Canyon we lived in a Navajo-style hogan with the great hogan bathroom down the hill. Meals were cafeteria-style, and the noise level in the dining room reflected the intensity and eagerness of the group. We chattered about our day in the lab or out on the digs with all of the other amateur archaeologists and had a marvelous time. The boys were the only teenagers in our bunch of about fifty. The genuine pleasure of unearthing a recognizable bit of pottery at least a thousand years old is one of life's special moments for all of us.

In every one of these excursions, the planning and organization by the Institution exceeded excellence.

Another group learning program is Elderhostel. Raving about Elderhostel has become a habit with me. By requesting their catalog (Elderhostel, 80 Boylston Street, Boston, MA 02116), any reader can find out about this remarkable program open to 60-plus "students." Participants live on campus in every state of the nation as well as abroad, studying subjects ranging from America's music to extraterrestrial intelligence. Price for one week, including room, board and tuition is just over $200 (1988 prices). I can't stay home for that.

"Cultures in Conflict," "Mythology and Science Fiction" and "Literature of the Southwest" were available as three one-hour lectures at the college of Santa Fe. Classroom discussion was extraordinary and stimulating, compared to our regular collegiate days. And again the people I met were marvelous. Next time I want to find a course in Greek dancing or maybe go to Scandinavia. There seems to be no limit to the variety of courses offered or the localities to explore.

This is going on all over the country, all over the world. Oldsters are finding a new lease on life through learning in programs specifically for retirees and through continuing education courses in community colleges. Some universities now offer *free* admission to senior citizens to audit college courses and participate in other programs.

Museums and organizations ranging from our local Hyde Collection in Glens Falls, New York, to the Metropolitan Museum of Art in New York City have entered into the group travel business. This is an excellent way to meet like-minded people who might appreciate many of the same sights around the country.

Notice too the travel opportunities offered by the National Trust for Historic Preservation, the Oceanic Society and other specific-interest outfits. Addresses are available at your local library.

So it goes. At any age and with any size crowd, you can be on the move, and never be alone. Or if just the two of you are looking for a hideaway . . . be my guest.

Is There a Way to Get There from Here?

Planes

Rodgers and Hammerstein told the truth: Everything *is* up to date in Kansas City. Especially at the airport. During my recent years of traveling around the world and elsewhere, airports have continually frustrated me. Most seem to be built for the convenience of the airlines, not the passengers. How can we send a person to the moon when my luggage can't make it through Dallas?

But Kansas City travelers have a heartening story to tell. Luggage is checked, loaded and unloaded at the boarding gates. Cross-country trudges to the baggage-claim area are nonexistent. Picture this: When my flight landed in Kansas

City, I walked up the ramp/tunnel to the terminal. Beside that gate, not 30 feet away, was a carousel unloading baggage from our flight. Immediately. The same was true when I boarded the flight back to Colorado. From the curbside entrance for *my* airline I went straight to the boarding gate, where I checked my luggage, which went without hesitation to my plane. That was a pleasure.

Another airport gaining more and more notice as one of the best anywhere is Tampa–St. Petersburg. It's a beauty. Marvelous high-speed monorails carry passengers from a central terminal building to smaller, manageable boarding terminals. Just follow simple directions and step in. The roomy car then zooms you over to wherever you're headed. One other observation about the Tampa airport: the food is excellent, particularly the seafood bar.

On the other end of the spectrum, at O'Hare in Chicago I dash from D14 to G53 in 45 minutes (no time for a "rest stop") to check in for a connecting flight. I might as well walk all the way from Albany.

And how about those confusing fare schedules? Some might sound great, but rely on your travel agent here. Some of these great-sounding premium offers have restrictions enough to choke a horse. Airline fares last less than two weeks. They change faster than a vaudeville chorus line. Fare schedules number in the hundreds between any two cities. Don't ask me why. The best approach is to question your agent adamantly:

What is the least expensive fare from Phoenix to Cleveland three weeks from now?

What are the restrictions?

What is the fare when I leave on March 31 and return April 12? If dates are inflexible, say so at once.

Is there a cancellation penalty?

What is the ticketing deadline?

Until what date will this fare be available?

Most important: Is this one of those frightful tickets absolutely unchangeable, nonrefundable and all that??? I have lost money thinking I would save by buying a crazy ticket which is not only useless but costly if my plans must be changed.

Once, a boarding attendant tried to refuse me a seat on a plane because I was using only the return portion of my ticket. She was undoubtedly right in accordance with their complicated regulations, but I told her I had reserved and paid for that seat on that plane, so I jolly well would go—I had already lost the fare for the first leg of the trip. She made some smart remark about how she was allowing me to fly on *her* airplane just because she was such a thoughtful, caring person. Truth was, I was bigger than she was, but I'll never again buy one of those lousy special-fare tickets, even though my best friends in the travel business insist upon trying to sell them to me.

I've learned about boarding planes too. The secret is don't be in such a hurry. By dashing up to the boarding chute on the very first call, you make your trip downright unpleasant before you ever leave the ground. Invariably there will be some who have sneaked through ahead of their row number and are jamming the aisles attempting to store their so-called carry-on luggage. Give those birds a chance to settle in and get out of your way. Then walk on easily and sit down. If you are wise enough to request an aisle seat, you can avoid getting up and down to let others into your row by boarding after your seatmates. That plane won't leave without you as long as you stay in the boarding area.

Pamela Fiori, editor of *Travel and Leisure*, has a wise word of caution. Says she, "Whatever I wear on the plane might end up being my wardrobe for the duration of the trip." Wrinkle-proof clothes and bright colors are suggested—and sensible shoes, of course.

One more packing thought occurs here. Full skirts. Women, if your most smashing or most comfortable outfit includes a full swinging skirt that looks terrible after being crushed in luggage, wear it on the plane. That way the skirt looks fine and so do you. Your in-transit outfit can also be a staple once you've reached your destination.

Another flight-time suggestion: walk up and down the aisle occasionally or do exercises at your seat, and avoid wearing support hose on long flights.

As for ear-popping: remember the good old days when stewardesses handed out chewing gum? You'll have to provide your own now, but that's still the best way to combat the annoyance and discomfort of popping ears. If that doesn't work, try holding your nose during ascent or descent or take a mild decongestant a half-hour or so before beginning your descent. Or stuff cotton in your ears for the flight.

If advice is what you are seeking in this book, here's the first dose: when you must fly, go to Kansas City or maybe Tampa. We'll consider more about flying, including a few hints that might prove helpful to you, in a later chapter. Right now, let's get on to other forms of transportation.

TRAINS

Certainly traveling by train takes more time, but train travel allows us to slow the pace a bit, to catch up with our own whirring lifestyles. That's the part I like best. What bothers most of those who refuse train travel is the demand for instant gratification. We have become an impatient society. We expect instant rice and microwave muffins. Left to our own devices for entertainment or trapped in solitude with our own thoughts, we have a tendency to be bored or jittery. That's too bad.

Around the world, trains offer affordable, convenient, usually dependable means of getting around. The most luxurious and most expensive are the Orient Express, of course, and the famous Blue Train, which travels between Durban and Capetown in South Africa. Those are top-drawer outfits. European and Japanese trains are considered superior to ours and with good reason in many instances. But those trains don't have as far to go as ours do. Not as many miles of track to tend.

European cities are close enough together to make flying unnecessary. So are the Japanese cities. It's safe to assume that in Europe, Japan and New Zealand train travel makes sense. Special tour rates are attractive, and the equipment is new and comfortable. Don't forget the best part about trains: they deposit you in the center of town and find their own parking spaces.

In Denmark, my travel-agent friend, Judy Smith, and I went to the Copenhagen train station and asked for a round-trip ticket to someplace—anyplace—for a five-or-six-hour trip. Local train. We wound up riding to Helsingor and back, but we could get off at any stop, look around and take the next train in our direction. After a fine luncheon and after smiling at a number of Danes and talking to a few, we returned to the hotel in Copenhagen, pleased that we'd seen more of that country than Tivoli Gardens and the statue of the mermaid.

In China the distances compare with those in the United States. Upgrading trains and modernizing them undoubtedly rates high priority in China's devotion to attracting tourists. But I do hope they won't scrap all of those charming old parlor cars with plush seats facing linen-laid tables set for tea. Chinese trains carry all sorts of vendors hawking wonders ranging from silk scarves and fans to jade and ivory pieces or calligraphic scrolls. That was great fun, even though the roadbed was rough at times.

On the Bullet Train in Japan, however, one of the vendors offering cold drinks sold me what must have been a sake cooler—or some soda I didn't appreciate. The cup was filled to the brim. Not knowing how to dispose of the stuff after tasting it, I simply set it on the floor beside my feet. That train traveled faster than a speeding bullet from Kyoto to Tokyo and not one drop from that cup was sloshed or spilled.

Incidentally, Judy Smith and I also rode the more ordinary trains in Japan, the inter-urbans, and had no trouble except for the fact we had way too much baggage for moving quickly on and off the trains. The wall-mounted route maps were understandable and people were more than helpful—except in giving us any help with our outrageous load of luggage.

How do American trains measure up? Let's talk about Amtrak. Of the people I know best, I have put in more Amtrak time than anyone. At least one or two trips every year since 1983, usually from Albany, New York, to La Junta, Colorado. Amtrak is not all bad. The secret of enjoying Amtrak is the decision to make getting there an integral part of the vacation.

IS THERE A WAY TO GET THERE FROM HERE?

The train, particularly if you have sleeping accommodations, is almost a decompression chamber.

Aboard Amtrak the meals are tasty and not expensive. Service is certainly less than expected in the good old days of Fred Harvey, but what does measure up to the good old days? One reason I prefer Amtrak over an airplane is the ease of boarding. And being met is almost no problem since I'm usually the only passenger getting off at La Junta, and my family has learned to check arrival time—since Amtrak is not as punctual as one might wish. By the end of the trip I have conversed with interesting people, enjoyed reading time to myself and thoroughly appreciated the lack of hassle that train travel affords.

My trip east to west takes 36 hours, five of which are in Chicago. Five hours at an airport miles from town is lost time. Five hours in downtown Chicago becomes a chance to visit the Art Institute, or the wondrous public library, or even Marshall Field's. With all of my Amtrak travel through Chicago, I've learned a lot about the city. At O'Hare for five hours I have learned nothing about anything.

Boarding the Southwest Chief, each passenger is presented a fine brochure featuring on-board activities and such: movies in the lounge car, an on-board guide to Indian Country, bingo and other games. There are four types of sleeping rooms, some with private bath. One, which must be a fancier room that I ever get, has a small danger: the push buttons for turning on the shower and for flushing the toilet are on the same panel. A woman at breakfast had all of us convulsed with laughter when she tried to describe her husband's hasty retreat from the bathroom fully dressed and drenched to the skin, thoroughly embarrassed about having pushed the wrong button. The economy bedroom serves my purpose well without such booby traps.

Morning on board Amtrak brings orange juice, coffee and a newspaper before breakfast. The Orient Express this is not, but for arriving well rested and at peace with my world, I don't know of anything that can beat it.

Besides that route of mine from Albany-Rensselaer to Colorado (and on out to Los Angeles), Amtrak offers tour rates and tour guides described in their *Travel Planner*. Hotel packages, tour packages, sightseeing services are spelled out. Just for instance, Amtrak's Boston and New England package costs as little as $228 (1988 prices) per person for four days, plus train fare: included are comprehensive sightseeing and choices of some of Boston's finest hotels. Or you might choose New Orleans or St. Louis or Las Vegas, or Whitefish, Montana, or San Simeon, California. Amtrak deserves your consideration.

FERRIES

Let's look at ferries. "Ferries?" you say. "Where am I going to ride a ferry?"

Sarah Bird Wright's new book, *Ferries of America*, answers that question. She lists 21 ferries in Massachusetts alone. All of them sound inviting. New York has more than 30 ferries in and around the city. We've all heard about midtown ferries in books or the movies. Heroes or shopgirls rode the Staten Island ferry. But have you heard of the Moro Bay ferry in Arkansas or the Rabbit Hash–Rising Sun ferry in Kentucky? This is where Sarah Wright's book shines. Listed are dozens of fascinating local ferries in existence for decades, unknown to most of us.

The South is a hotbed of wonderfully named ferries: for example, in North Carolina, the *Ocracoke-Swan Quarter* and the *Governor Edward Hyde*. The *Hyde* crosses Pamlico Sound on the Outer Banks with 30 cars and 300 passengers in two and a half hours.

Ferries abound in the Great Lakes region and the upper Midwest too. On the Detroit River steamships built at the turn of the century, the *Columbia* and the *Ste. Claire*, ferry 2,500 passengers apiece to Boblo Island Amusement Park. The park is even older than the ships. And here's the best part. Round-trip fare on the ferry includes unlimited roller-coaster rides and access to all other attractions in the amusement park. I'm getting to Detroit soon as I can to try that one. Then I'll ride the *Catawba Point–Put in Bay* in Ohio, or perhaps the *Merrimac-Okee* in Wisconsin.

Ferries of the West are equally fascinating: in Galveston, Texas; Wheatland, Oregon; California—crossing San Francisco Bay or carrying funlovers to Catalina Island. Utah claims to have the highest ferry, at 3,700 feet. The *John Atlantic Burr* is a new ship crossing Lake Powell at the historic point used by explorers and settlers to cross the Colorado River. It is part of the Utah highway system and has opened up much of the rugged country of southern Utah to tourists. Another dandy idea for tripping in the Southwest.

Now about the Northwest. Washington State ferries are legendary. Says Sarah Bird Wright, "The ships have amenities which astonish outsiders used to more mundane forms of mass transit." Some of these ferries have duty-free shops, since they are international carriers. Ferries provide communication and transportation along the 2,000 miles of densely wooded coastline of Washington State. Exploring and trying out the wonders of Washington ferries would make a worthwhile vacation in itself.

Alaska has every other state beat by a country mile in this department, thanks to the water transportation system known as the Alaska Marine Highway. This makes for a summertime expedition unmatched around the world, with the possible exception of the fjords of Norway. Again I quote from *Ferries of America*, "There are few better ways to view the massive thick-ribbed glaciers, foaming waterfalls, ice-topped dark mountains and icebergs starkly jutting from the gray water than to ride the state's unique ferry system." How about that?

For me, opening this book is stepping into a new world. Because of it, I've enjoyed the ferries on Lake Champlain between New York and Vermont and those around Vancouver, San Francisco, or Balboa, California, as well as European ferries. Before reading parts of this treasure-trove, I had thought there were no ferries across the Mississippi River. I had tried to find one when I was planning a drive with grandchildren from upstate New York to Colorado and had come up blank. But the index has 15 references for ferries crossing the Mississippi. Next time. Now that I have the book.

Almost any ferry-finding trip would be a good project with grandchildren. For instance, in Rhode Island the ferry from Providence to Newport to Block Island crosses Naragansett Bay. The vessel is the *Nelesco*, built in 1981. Description of local points of interest runs a full page in Sarah's book. A ferry a day would be a marvelous variation on the usual sightseeing agenda for travelers of all ages.

The ferry I love most on Lake Champlain has been in service since 1825—not the same vessel, but serving the same purpose. Lake Champlain is 120 miles long. The east shore of Champlain is sometimes referred to as the "West Coast of New England," and so it must have seemed 200 years ago. Four ferries operate across this "sixth Great Lake." Northernmost is the one I often take from Plattsburg, New York, to Grand Isle and the Hero Islands of Vermont. This is a short trip, but it's fun to stand by the rail in summer to watch the boats on the lake. In February a friend and I felt like Little Eva escaping from Simon Legree dodging ice floes in our path. The ice of the north country was impressive, but the vessel never faltered.

Colorado is a wonderful place to live or visit, but we cannot boast about ferries. So whenever Westerners choose to visit me while I am in Lake George, New York, my first "guided tour" is Ausable Chasm, then to Port Kent for the hour-long ferry ride to Burlington, Vermont. After testing one of the fine restaurants in Burlington, we stop in at the Shelburne Museum, then head south for either the Charlotte–Essex ferry or the Ticonderoga ferry to get back on the New York side. Not only do these ferry crossings make the day special for my guests, but they also recall prerevolutionary history with practically a hands-on feeling.

Out West everyone's talking about the ferry service at Bullhead City, Arizona. Bullhead City? That's just up the road from Needles, California, one of the desert spots of the world—and there's a ferry there? As a matter of fact, Bullhead City has *lots* of ferries. Plying the sometimes shallow, sometimes turbulent waters of the Colorado River is a whole fleet of tiny ferryboats. Each carries no more than 30 passengers—free.

Bullhead City lies across the Colorado River from Laughlin, Nevada. On the Arizona banks of the river, motels and parking lots seem to make up most of the town. Everything here is brand new; this is no revival of some old mining town. This entire operation appears to be the brain-child of one man, Don Laughlin—"Donald Trump of the Desert," perhaps. Opposite Arizona's parking lots and motels, on the Nevada side of the river, stands the most amazing line-up of casinos west of Atlantic City. You must see it to believe it. One casino looks like a huge sternwheeler riverboat, others are equally imaginative. Small-scale Las Vegas is what we have here, but Las Vegas can't boast of public transportation equal to this ferry system.

Why the ferries? That's the way the towns work. Vacationers apparently check into motels on the Arizona side, then park their cars in the lot facing a particularly lucky-looking gambling establishment across the river. From each parking lot is an inviting stairway to a small dock. Stand on the dock for a minute or two and up glides a canopied ferry boat. You hop on and ride to the casino on the other side. You can walk from any casino to another—and therefore try the slots all up and down the river. Then when the nickels or quarters run out, you reboard the ferry to your car and go on off to bed.

This is absolutely relaxed, casual and generally pleasant. There are many more nickel slot machines per gambler in Laughlin than I have noticed in Reno, Las Vegas or Atlantic City. And almost no high-stakes baccarat games to be seen. I hit one machine for 100 quarters. Is it any wonder I think Bullhead/Laughlin is fun?

Ferryboats lead us into another, newer world of water travel: ferryliners. Ferryliners have been common in European waterways for years. North Americans are just now getting into the act. The whole concept sounds fascinating and practical. Michael and Laura Murphy's book, *Ferryliner Vacations in North America: Ocean Travel and Inland Cruising*, is the authority on the subject. "Ferryliner companies operate 22 long-sea ships ranging from 3,000 to 15,000 gross tons capable of carrying up to 1,500 passengers along some of the most beautiful routes in the world and between some of the most delightful port towns and cities in the world," according to the authors.

Along the coasts of Mexico, British Columbia, Alaska, the eastern seaboard and in the inland waterways, these ships are more and more numerous, more and more popular. The Murphys' book tells us about connections, condition of the ships, quality of food and service, accommodations, rates and much more about the world of port-to-port travel.

What's so great about ferryliners? First of all, taking the car along on the ship enables us to cruise one way and then drive back, which often makes sense. Next, port stays are optional. If Puerto Vallarta looks and feels like heaven-on-earth to you, ferryliners allow you the flexibility of staying there extra days (drive your car around the countryside) and then buying another ticket for your return trip or for journeying on down the coast. Particularly in low-travel seasons, setting your own cruise schedule becomes a reality. Passengers are not bound to buy the entire cruise itinerary.

Stopovers along your route can be arranged before leaving home if you wish, or buying one leg of a trip at a time might seem a better idea. Either way sounds appealing, since fares are generally lower than for regular cruise ships, and dress codes more relaxed.

Ferryliners sound totally fascinating to me—way up there on my High Priority Travel List. Maine or Mexico? Alaska or Baja? The choices abound.

One more point about this compendium of ferryliner information. The Murphys have included basic data about the New York state canal system.

The "in" crowd does a lot of talking about their barge trips in France, which must be memorable experiences. I often wonder if those same people know about barge canals in our own Northeast. I certainly intend to take advantage of these opportunities in the near future. That's beautiful country we're talking about here.

IS THERE A WAY TO GET THERE FROM HERE?

The Mid-Lakes Navigation Company of Skaneateles, New York, offers three-to-six-day cruises on various stretches of the New York state canal system. Did you know that? Between Albany and Buffalo on the Erie Canal, between Albany and Whitehall on the Champlain Canal of the Hudson River, and on the Cayuga-Seneca and the Oswego canals passengers enjoy leisurely trips through interesting lock systems and legendary country. Accommodations on shore are included in the overall fare, as are all meals. There are also day cruises on unbelievably scenic Lake Skaneateles. And enough variety of tripping available to please every appetite, to satisfy every whim.

Check Your Tires and Tauck about Bus Tours

Auto Traveling

"Two-week vacation? Who needs it? I spent two weeks in a car with John Weaver's kids in one afternoon." That's what John's Uncle Joe remarked after driving from Kansas City to Concordia, Kansas, with our three little darlings, ages one to five.

Any mention of family travel by car brings the same memories to all of us: restless youngsters fighting over comic books in the back seat; car-sick dogs and wet babies who finally fall asleep five miles from the place you hoped to stop at for lunch; arguments over which radio station sounds worst; attempts to play games like Car Bingo or Billboard Alphabet with everyone accused of cheating.

Since our days of (1) being the kid in the back seat, or (2) being the parent in charge of these endurance contests, we should have learned a lot about simplifying automobile touring. Basically, that's what we all need: simplifying.

Back in the thirties my parents used to load us all into the biggest Buick they could afford, since there were four of us sisters to compete for control of the back seat. Usually we were headed from Kansas to California for summertime visits with Grandfather and cousins. From the time we left the home driveway before dawn (so as to get as far as possible before the heat of the day turned our pre-air-conditioned car into a rolling sauna) until we crossed the desert into Blythe or Needles in California, Mother and Dad must have been close to crazy.

Life on the road is certainly more comfortable now. Cars don't go any faster, but motels have sprung up, interstate highways have been cut across most states like giant skid marks from one end to the other, and air conditioning and cruise control have made both the driver and the passengers more relaxed, if not more pleasant. Gone are the days when radiators boiled over at the side of the road. Flat tires are a different story from the blowouts I remember from childhood outings.

What is there to interfere with enjoying a day trip, weekend or long vacation in our cars? First, let's examine attitudes. We want instant gratification. Headed for Las Vegas or Fort Lauderdale, most of us want to get there as quickly as possible, little realizing the overland journey in itself can be a real vacation. Just as this Get-There-as-Quickly-as-We-Can syndrome is responsible for impatience with the trains, so it is with car travel.

It's an old story: The woman on the plane who explained, "Last year we didn't go to Florida. We were in Majorca."

"So where's Majorca?"

"I don't know, we flew."

There are better ways to learn about the world.

Often, flying to our chosen spot and renting a car is only sensible, but if you are my age and time is what you have the most of, then traveling mile-by-mile with congenial companions in your car is economical and a joy. Plus, you stand to learn a lot along the way.

"Sit in that Ford all the way to the East Coast? You must be slap-happy. I tried that once. The kids cried, the car was a mess of crumbs and soda cans, we never stopped until we were almost out of gas. Plus, we were lost in the middle of Boston."

Or, "Who'd want to ride with a bunch of old women for a week? All they'll talk about is their bladder trouble and their stupid sons-in-law. And they'd never agree about where to stay or how much to spend for lunch. And the driving is a chore. And my knees get so they won't bend."

That identifies the subjects to be thought over here. Before you or I get out in the middle of the San Luis Valley or somewhere along the Mohawk Trail and decide, as my grandson did years ago, "Oma, next time you say, 'Jason, do you want to go on a picnic?' I hope I'll say NO," let's make the practical observations and decisions. Let's plan a better picnic.

These suggestions are meant for those readers who have felt the same trepidations as I once did: "Can I manage well enough to go driving around the country without a guide, a group or a keeper maybe?"

Recognizing the obvious advantages of car travel—economy, flexibility, convenience—we should:

1. Concentrate on short jaunts at first.
2. Have a well-defined reason for the trip.
3. Plan routes, stops and attractions carefully.
4. Understand your car and its maintenance.
5. Choose companions with care.
6. Avoid midseason or weekend travel.
7. Look for pleasure more than convenience.
8. Make essential money decisions before leaving home.
9. Remember "scenic" is more rewarding than "shorter" sometimes.
10. Look for new pleasures; don't stick with the "old days."

Having lined ourselves up that much, we can begin. Enthusiasm will build as plans take shape, believe me.

1. CONCENTRATE ON SHORT JAUNTS AT FIRST, particularly if you are unsure about this whole idea. The way I picture it is three or four people getting together to travel no

more than one day's drive away. Overnight is a good test for those of us who haven't traveled together before. Read carefully the regional news in your daily newspaper. Is there a special exhibition in a nearby museum? A performance you'd enjoy in a restored theater? A Broadway play has come to the city, but you don't want to drive home alone at night?

Without waiting for the inclination, the time or the money to leave on a week-long vacation, good friends just pick up and go. In so doing, they create a break in their routine and something new to think about.

2. PICK OUT ONE "SPECIAL INTENTION." Craft displays, ski lessons, hot-air balloon festivals, summer concerts, poetry readings, nouvelle cuisine, the birthplace of a president or the commemoration of a battle. These are examples of reasons to get out of your routine long enough to find out what's going on out there. Particularly important are the events we know nothing about. That's learning in the best sense of the word.

3. PLAN CAREFULLY TO AVOID this kind of scenario: "Okay? Let's go. I'll pick you up at ten o'clock. Shall we call Margaret? Or Betty? This will be such fun. We'll just do it!" That conversation is often followed by, "Do you know the way?" which can lead to real trouble and discouragement before the plan ever gets off the ground.

Far better to say, "Let's take some time right now to look at the map," even if you've been there many times. My friend Regina and I have been in Troy, New York, a dozen times. We can get in all right, but every time we head out of town, one of us says, "Here comes the part where we get lost. I hate it when that happens." One of these days we'll take our own advice and identify the road out of Troy in advance.

Another depressing circumstance is attempting to read maps in the dark. You know the scene: one opens the glove compartment to squint at the red line showing which direction I-25 is supposed to go, the back seater always remarks we should learn to carry flashlights, the driver, in despair, flicks on the dome light for the "navigator" but then can't see to drive. Eventually, you stop to ask directions, but by this time it's later than you intended and tempers are shortened.

Planning a motor trip should always begin with a careful assessment of the size of the trunk of the car. There might not be room for three hairdryers and a hamper for the teapot and the traveling percolator. One extra pair of good walking shoes per passenger might be the limit. While you are measuring the trunk space, notice too how the spare tire is stored, and where the tools are kept.

Planning attractions means consideration of the interests and tastes of the tour participants. If you're headed for a pre-revolutionary house museum and Shirley has no desire to look at such old stuff, don't expect Shirley to come along and go into ecstasy over Fort Ticonderoga. Include Shirley on the next trip to the city, and invite Charlotte this time. She loves old cannons and Indian relics.

Naturally there will be mistakes. I'll never live down the hotel reservations I arranged with the clerk on the phone who assumed I meant two beds when I asked for "two doubles." What I wanted was two double rooms for four of us. Happily, my buddies on that New Mexico outing were good sports and made an hysterical two days out of cramped quarters. Nice gals, but that taught me to be more precise when making reservations by phone.

4. NOBODY REALLY EXPECTS EVERY CAR OWNER to understand what goes on under the hood. We should have sense enough, however, to know when our cars need the oil changed or the snow tires put on. We trust those poor machines to keep right on humming along without much attention, and most manage pretty well, but before you head out of town, away from your friendly Mr. Goodwrench, go through the check-up routine. Find out what weight oil you should ask for.

Belonging to any reputable auto club is practical and smart; towing can be a real hassle, especially in a strange place, so having ready reference to AAA or Mobil or other auto club is a face-saver. For an extended motor trip, you might even consider renting a car and sharing expenses. That way, if you run into any kind of car trouble, Hertz or Avis can either fix it or supply a working model. That saves your good car at home.

5. CHOOSE COMPANIONS WITH CARE. We've discussed this a bit, as far as mutual interests are concerned. The friend who is most welcome at the bridge table or the Rotary Club meetings is not necessarily the best traveling companion. One night out for the first trip is the best test. Conversation for three hours in a car gets old unless you all have common concerns.

This doesn't mean your travel pals should be clones of yourself. It does mean everyone in the party ought to have the same relative sense about money, about time and about what the purpose of the excursion is. The least welcome companion on any trip is the man or woman who cannot get places on time. Keeping the rest of the gang waiting while you re-do your nails or make up your mind about which framed print to buy is inexcusable unless the whole crowd behaves in the same way. If they do, you deserve each other.

6. IF YOU ARE RETIRED, YOU CAN REMEMBER when we had to do our tripping on weekends or holidays because the kids were in school and jobs made weekday meandering impossible. Too often we find ourselves stuck to that pattern even though it is no longer a necessity. Some fares are cheaper midweek, some hotel rates are better in off-season. Taking advantage of our greater latitude in spending our leisure time makes sense both by saving money and avoiding crowds. Next time you are tempted to say, "What are you doing next weekend?" bite your tongue. Then say, "What are you doing on Tuesday and Wednesday? Shall we get away for a day or two?"

7. LOOK FOR PLEASURE more than convenience. This applies to bed-and-breakfast outings or riding on bumpy narrow-gauge trains, or walking some distance to get to the ruins of an old mission. You can be comfortable and accommodated in every way back home. What you came here to see and to learn is more important than having air-conditioned everything and the right spoon for your soup. Above all, this is the step that means, *Do Not Complain*, unless something is mightily wrong and not as advertised. Enjoy the change in your surroundings, if only because home will look so much better when you get back.

8. MAKE DECISIONS ABOUT MONEY before leaving home. One of my "harping" ideas is about handling money. That's why this step is important. If you're going to split luncheon checks and share car expenses equally, then put the funds together in equal shares and do not worry about who had more for dinner or who ate the biggest breakfast. One of your group can handle this without everyone at the table fishing for extra change or five people all trying to pay for the drinks at once. Decide too how much this will cost, including theater tickets, museum admissions, whatever. Then stick to the group budget. Playing by the rules—that's the way to have the most fun, and the gang will ask you to go again.

9. "SCENIC" OFTEN YIELDS GREATER RETURNS than "shorter" or "faster." Getting off the interstate is a most valuable decision on almost any drive. Some interstate highways are beautiful, like the Northway through the Adirondacks up to the Canadian border, but that's an exception. Outstanding scenery is preserved along older country roads where a connection with the life of the area still exists.

The *Reader's Digest* has published a book, *Off the Beaten Path*, which lists more than 1,000 scenic places "still uncrowded and inviting." We'll talk more about that later. The *Tour Books* from AAA are also aimed at out-of-the-heavy-traffic routes when possible. Side trips are recommended along the major highways, too. Harriet Webster has written a little guide book, *Favorite Short Trips in New York State*, for the *Yankee* Magazine Guidebook Series. These and literally hundreds more guides are available in libraries and bookstores. The bibliography in this book is an attempt to draw your attention to some of the better ones, and my example of how to use these works for your own planning comes later in this chapter.

10. THIS IS THE MOST IMPORTANT POINT I'd like to make about touring on our own with friends: search out the new, the untried. Hanging onto the past when we venture forth can lead to the disappointments of rundown hotels, overgrown resorts and overbuilt quaint villages.

Once I insisted that my husband and I take a side trip to see Red River, New Mexico, which, in my childhood, had been a cluster of two hotels and a grocery store, with all the charm of real mountain country. The first sight greeting us as we approached this veritable paradise was the huge slag dump of a molybdenum mine. Don't do that to yourself. Red River might be all right for some folks now, but my going back to capture the good old days was a fatal mistake.

Where can we go in our cars in a day or two to lift us out of the doldrums and make life sparkle again? Here's a game I claim to have invented: Spread the road map of your state on the dining room table, so several of you can see it at once. Then circle your hometown with a radius of about 300 miles. The lid of your vitamin/calcium wide-mouth bottle is the right size. Study what's in that circle for your short-trip enjoyment. The circles would be like those "Guess Where?" puzzles that used to be in the *Saturday Evening Post.*

Here's one excursion I found inside the circle I drew around my hometown of Pueblo, Colorado. Remember, close to home is what we tend to overlook. For 33 years, I have been a southern Coloradoan. For 33 years I have ignored the museum in Cañon City. Miss Sarah, her friend, Autumn, and I discovered this museum on the second floor of the municipal building when we were driving around just for fun. Indescribable. The collection is well cared for, nicely displayed, and the most eclectic assortment of stuff I have encountered in one place.

The Zulu war club is mounted on a wall next to the Canadian moose. Not ten feet away a Japanese machine gun is aimed at the heart of Teddy Roosevelt. Over the fireplace built of petrified femurs and other rock formations are suspended snowshoes and a model birchbark canoe. Pottery made by world-renowned Maria of San Ildefonso Pueblo shares a shelf in a display case with dressed fleas under a magnifying glass. A stuffed bobcat crouches atop another row of shelves, in anticipation of a mighty leap at a leather-winged bat in flight. Seashells, geodes, arrowheads, combs made of almost anything, harness bells, stuffed bison, and *Ben-Hur, A Story of Christ* in Braille; all safe under one roof.

We're not talking "dusty" here. This collection is arranged for public enjoyment and enlightenment with as much concern as any exhibit in the Smithsonian. As a matter of strict fact, that's what I'm reminded of here. The Arts and Industries Building at the Smithsonian has such a wide variety of artifacts and memorabilia on display. The principal difference is that your feet don't get so tired in those three rooms in Cañon City and you avoid crowds.

Miss Sarah and Autumn honestly were ecstatic. "Oma, come look at this. Oma, did you see these beautiful rocks? Oma, these arrowheads are so little—and so big!" They were most fascinated with the dressed fleas, most impressed with the antlers on a gigantic elk and the horns on a cape buffalo. These fifth-graders recognized the porcupine-quill decoration on the oldest of the moccasins and sat on the chair made of antlers.

Almost any small town anywhere has a museum worth our attention. Cañon City is not unique, just close to my home. Back in the days when one or two families in a "little mining town in the West" had the distinction of being the folks who had been to Europe, travelers would bring back all of these wonders to share with the hometown: Chinese tea sets, Japanese fans, native costumes, all for the school children to see (like the dead whale on a flat car which was hauled into our town in Kansas once a year for the school children to see for a dime).

One relic bothered me: a row of school desks with fold-up seats exactly like the ones we sat in at Roosevelt School. Why would anyone think those were old enough to be put in a museum?

Playing the 300-mile circle game from Augusta, Georgia, for example, there are enough "scenic and interesting places still uncrowded and inviting" to keep you on the go for weeks— one or two days at a time. Intriguing names, "Dahlonega Courthouse Gold Museum," "Uncle Remus Museum," "Cumberland Island National Seashore," fill the pages of *Off the Beaten Path*, and that's a fraction of the listings inside the Augusta circle. In the Carolinas, within a day's drive are Carl Sandburg's home, North Carolina's Reed Gold Mine, and no fewer than 17 wonders to behold in South Carolina.

Off the Beaten Path discloses centers of attraction in four states if you're lucky enough to live in Albert Lea, Minnesota.

From Albany, New York, the circle encloses parts of seven states where sightseeing starts with Montour Falls ("Almost as high as Niagara. . . spectacular in summer and sparkling with sheets of ice in winter") and winds up in Connecticut, Rhode Island, Massachusetts (Saugus Iron Works or John Alden's house are only two of more than 20 designated spots).

You get the idea. Create an itinerary of your own interests. Do not neglect, however, the excellent guides for hiking and day-tripping now available in bookstores and libraries. You'll find examples listed in Chapter 10.

One last pointer about cars. Do you recall my little dialogue earlier about how "My knees get so they won't bend"? Well here's the best advice you'll find about that: *Wherever you are, stop along the road every 100 miles to walk around, stretch and change drivers on a regular rotation system.* Promise me you'll do that. Then I'll be certain you'll have a wonderful time.

Bus Tours

"What about bus tours?" you're saying to yourself. "This woman has discussed ships, trains, ferries, cars—what about buses?" Certainly one of the most popular forms of sightseeing and vacation travel is by motor coach, whether you sign on alone, with a friend or in a crowd. With today's wide-window coaches—commodious, comfortable and fully equipped—there's no reason a motor tour here or abroad cannot be a satisfying experience.

Leading tour companies, such as Tauck Tours and Maup-intour, have been in this business for years and have earned the finest of reputations. To see fall foliage, the Grand Canyon, Cape Cod, the battlefields of the Civil War or any of hundreds of other wonders of the world, escorted tours make sense.

Before signing up for what appears to be the bargain of the ages, however, do keep in mind that you'll probably get just what you pay for. Examine the fine print about how many meals are included and what sort of accommodations are provided along the way. Tour buses coming into Lake George are parked at the best and the worst of places. I've seen bus passengers lined up outside an el cheapo cafe for long waits for bad food at the same time other busloads of folks are being given the best of food and service down the street.

The best motor tours, in my opinion, are those organized by tour planners who pick a central hotel/motel as a "hub" for two or three days of sightseeing, instead of forcing passengers to pack up every morning before breakfast and drag suitcases into different rooms every night along the way. An extra advantage to this kind of planning is obvious: anyone wanting to "take a day off" to spend time on their own can do so.

With this genre of tourism, my experience is twofold, so the tables are turning here. I plan to tell you how the customers look to the tour conductors, since I have spent almost equal time being the "conductor" and the "conductee."

The worst passengers on any motor coach tour, be it on a New England fall foliage tour or a tour of the Grand Tetons, are those devils who are always late. You've seen them. From the first call to get going in the morning until the last stop at night, the same bums are the last to board the bus. And they don't care. They dawdle over coffee after showing up at the last minute for breakfast. Then they have to get their luggage, which should have been picked up forty minutes ago. All day long the tour director is saying, "Please, Mr. Lagalong, the bus is waiting." But it's no use. They pay no attention to schedules, take twenty minutes for ten minutes of picture-taking, handle every souvenir in every shop without buying anything and then disappear after lunch.

Almost (but not quite) worse than Mr. or Ms. Lagalong is the Front Seat Hog. This guy (women can be just as obnoxious) plants himself in the seat behind the driver as soon as the door is opened for the first time, then acts as if Divine Right has decreed that seat to be his for eternity—or at least until the group returns to Cleveland. Nothing but a selfish child, this guy glares at anyone who suggests the front seat might be shared. Even when the director decrees rotation of seating, the Front Seat Hog claims some reason to stay put.

From my limited experience as a tour director, even I can tell you these are the two people the director would rather see under the bus than aboard it. You can spot them a mile away.

Camera buffs are sometimes a pain too. Tour organizers cringe when they spy a tripod coming aboard. There was a self-important man with an expensive-looking camera on board a ship with me once. That crabby old man yelled at anyone who made the mistake of walking within range of his viewfinder— as if he owned the Andes or at least had exclusive rights to look at them. When he bellowed at me, "If you walk in front of my camera once more, I'm going to kick you," I crept out of his way like a whipped dog, but the other travelers within ear shot let him have it. People like that make tour directing a bum job.

Then there's the smart aleck who knows more than the guides. Probably this clown was here once before, back in '54 or during the war. No statement of the guide goes unchallenged. Anyone else trying to listen to the narration en route to the pagoda or hot springs or burial mound is subjected to Mr. Know-It-All's caustic comments. This disruptive character has also stayed in better hotels, eaten in finer restaurants, seen higher waterfalls and deeper canyons than anyone else on the bus. This type can be easily spotted because they often wear stupid hats, and their jackets are covered with pins and souvenir patches meant to impress the rest of us.

"Now wait just a minute," you're saying. "These unpleasant people show up on all travels, not just bus tours." True. But the group traveling in one bus is a closer community than that on a train or a ship—or even a ferry.

What to do if one of these pests is signed up on your tour? Easy. Move to the back of the bus. That very back seat is the best seat. You can turn around to get a full-circle view of the scenery. Generally, nobody fights for those seats. Often there's a back door, so boarding is no problem. Picture-taking is better back there, and you can sneak a candy bar or some cookies without feeling guilty about not sharing.

Evaluating the promotion of a bus tour or any travel package involves a careful study of the hotels offered. Those brochures that say something like "first-rate accommodations" without naming names could turn out to be promoting this year's Fleabag Special.

For me, the hotel is as important as the bus or the scenery—ideally the hotel chosen for your group should be as nice as you would choose on your own. Service, rooms, convenience of location of any hotel can make or break a trip.

Your travel agent can be a real help in evaluating any tours, especially motor tours. Your neighbors' experience and your own good sense will help, too. Pack only what you can carry, and be prepared to "play the game." You'll find many new friends and great adventure when you leave the driving to those other guys.

Over the Waves or around the Bend

OCEAN-LINER CRUISES

"Well, what shall we do today? What's going on?"

"How can I make up my mind this early in the morning?
Have you looked at the schedule for today? You didn't tell me
there'd be so much I'd want to do, or that we'd stay up so late
so often because the shows are so great. But I'll start with the
low-impact aerobics, then go to the bridge lecture at ten."

"Okay, but you'll miss the lecture about Barbados in the
theater. I'd rather go to the pool exercises. Then I'll be ready for
the blackjack tournament after lunch on the deck."

"Speaking of the deck, why don't we both go sit in the sun
and forget all this other stuff?"

"You've got it!"

The time has come to discuss cruises.

Leading the two of us, you and me, through the maze of travel advantages, opportunities and options turns out to be more of a challenge than I had anticipated.

For years now I have collected travel trivia and memorabilia. Guide books, museum catalogs, maps, note pads, ships' newspapers, magazines, brochures and thousands of ragged sheets salvaged from the travel pages of the *New York Times* are piled all over the place. These have been tentatively sorted and resorted into stacks labeled "Walking Tours," "Exotic Trips," "Tips" and such.

This is my filing system. My dining room table disappeared under my "files" years ago, and has been seen only on holidays and family festival occasions. Once in a while I rearrange the files by moving the mess to the guest room or the kitchen counters. Right now the stacks are cleverly balanced on chairs, cardboard boxes and upside-down wastebaskets in the workroom. The slipperiest, bulkiest tower of papers, paper clips and rubber bands is marked "Cruises."

That one hoard of valuable information takes hours to sort through, because every scrap is fun to read all over again. I love cruises. For almost 20 years I have been clutching this treasure trove of cruise information, savoring each minute recalled.

Cruising attracts more customers every day and is more popular now than ever. "The number of people taking cruises has doubled since 1982," says Janet Lynch in the December 1987 issue of *Travel and Leisure*. The primary reason for this increase is cruise life itself.

Once on board ship, we unpack and never hassle with luggage or money again until we disembark. My friend Sydney liked to compare being on board a Royal Viking ship to being submerged in warm water—being totally comfortable and cared for. Food, service, entertainment, transportation and lodging are all provided on board this one vessel. There's no need to worry about which restaurant to choose or which hotel to try. Purchases on board, drinks, tips are all payable at one time. Maybe one of the greatest attractions of cruise life is being rid of the constant attending to money. That, incidentally, is the reason cruise fares seem higher than other sorts of vacations—you pay for almost everything all at once.

Just as is true with the rest of the world, in choosing a cruise line we generally get what we pay for. There are variations in the quality of food and service; that's to be expected and to be studied ahead of time. Size and capacity of the ships vary, too. A crowded ship might cost less, but it's harder to find a place to stand by the rail, or the hot tub can be overflowing with little kids.

Fearful of mal de mer? *Travel and Leisure* magazine offers these pointers. Try to choose a cabin midships and near the water line. Ask your doctor about the skin patches from which the seasick medicine is absorbed into the bloodstream. (Such medication should be used with caution, of course.) On board ship, stay on deck; fresh air helps. Inside, lie on your back with eyes closed. In or out, fix your eyes on a distant object; don't lean over the rail and watch the ocean rushing by. Avoid alcohol, tobacco and too much rich food. In other words, easy does it.

Nevertheless, the real magic of being on a cruise is being out on the water. Not much can please me as completely as standing on an open deck watching the wake behind us. Once in a while a flying fish darts over the surface, or a porpoise makes a Sea-World leap alongside. Someone generally claims to have seen whales, which keeps me glued to that one spot for hours. The stern of a ship is one of the world's best spots for flying a kite.

Speaking of kite flying—here's one of my favorite stories.

Cary Grant, his gorgeous young wife and I took a cruise together—the three of us and 500 or 600 other passengers. Unlike many celebrity guests the Grants mingled with their fellow travelers and took an active part in shipboard life: sing-alongs around the piano and all that. They even played bingo and took dance lessons.

You should have seen him. Even in the morning he was Cary Grant. The accent, the manner, the tone of voice, the

charm never slipped. He was nearly 80 then, in 1983. His figure was trim; his posture perfect. He was not cutesy-smiley,
just pleasant.

My kites interested him. I had several with me and collected more along the way from Hong Kong to Durban. One
breezy day I was on the promenade deck at the stern of the ship
messing with a Chinese kite. It was a silk phoenix bird which
fluttered, soared, dipped and shuddered in the combination of
cross-winds and hot air from the ship's engines. I would launch
the kite on the port side trying to keep it clear of railings, deck
chairs and a few passengers. That feisty devil of a kite would
dance around where I wanted it for a few minutes, dive
dangerously close to the water, then invariably fly toward the
center of the deck, flirting with the flagpole. For two hours or
more I stayed there totally absorbed in the air currents, the
challenge of the unruly kite, the varying tugs on the line. I
never let it out more than 200 feet and had a marvelous time.

Once in a while I looked back toward the upper decks of the
ship and noticed a couple leaning against the rail on the highest
passenger deck. They waved at me, the stunning young woman
and the tanned, elegant man with snow-white hair and black-
rimmed glasses. I waved back.

That evening, Cary Grant stopped at my table in the dining
room. "You had a marvelous duel with that kite today. Barbara
and I were fascinated watching you." Now *that* has to be the
switch of the century: Cary Grant was watching *me*.

Watching birds on board ship can be fascinating, too. On
any cruise ship there are at least five major species to be ob-
served: the boasters, the shiners, the socialites, the dirvishes
and the laid-back amiables. The laid-back amiables generally
outnumber the other species but are less conspicuous because
of their unruffled feathers.

Subspecies abound, particularly on a ship that offers 50 different activities daily, four or five bars, and at least a dozen
feeding times every day. Easiest to spot are the *two-fisted
barflies*. These perchers stake out claims on the center stools of
the most popular bars (usually aft, near the swimming pool),
and stay there for the duration. There is general disagreement

about whether or not these birds ever sleep. Apparently they never leave their posts, much like male hummingbirds guarding their sugar-water feeders. The call of the subspecies is easily recognized: "Set 'em up again," at frequent intervals.

Seldom seen at the bar are the *glassy-eyed gluttonbirds*. These gobblers spend every waking moment hovering over food—any food. Beginning with an early-risers' breakfast, then a dining room breakfast, then the late-risers' breakfast, these birds follow this behavior pattern for 18 hours. They never miss tea, the boullion breaks, cake decorating demonstrations, or the midnight buffet. They waddle off the ship picking their teeth, burping and muttering about getting their money's worth.

More strenuous are the *deep-breathing deck-striders*. These on-board athletes log five or ten miles around the deck, counting laps. There is a congenital fear of smiling among these birds.

Less dedicated to exercise are the *eight-o'clock groaners*. This is my crowd. We commiserate, bending and stretching while the macho young man who is our leader shakes his head and sighs.

Golden-grilled suncatchers are as immobile as the deck-striders are active. Should they move too much, they'd slide off the afterdeck; they're so drenched in oil.

Beagle-voiced bitchers are few in number, but have the strongest homing instincts. They hover around the maître d' and swarm in clockwise gyrations around the cruise director.

Strictly nocturnal are the *sequin-breasted strutters* followed by the *black-tie grouches*. Their mating ritual consists of carefully counted cha-cha steps or Arthur Murray waltz routines. In contrast to the deck-striders, these birds have smiles painted on.

Despite the size of current ocean-liner cruise ships, some cruise lines are building even bigger ships than are now in service. I guess they want to appeal to all possible tastes in the cruising world. The new *Sovereign of the Seas* (Royal Caribbean Cruise Line) will be 73,000 tons with fourteen decks and a five-story central lobby. The Norwegian Caribbean Line's new giant, *Seaward*, is also termed a megaship.

Bigger ships are a matter of personal preference certainly. This country girl found it hard to be comfortable on the *Queen Elizabeth II*, since it compares in size to downtown Dallas. The *Norway* is even larger. It's easy to get lost. I had the feeling some passengers never found the right dining room or wandered for five days hunting for their cabin.

"I'm damned if I'm going to go on a vacation where I have to wear a tuxedo or dress like Little Lord Fauntleroy for breakfast." That's a common complaint about taking a cruise—having to stay dressed up all the time. Ships today are not as dressy as the old *Kungsholm* or original *Queen Elizabeth* used to be. Life on board is more casual. Still, on most of the classier cruises, passengers are expected to dress for dinner on full days at sea. The ship's daily newspaper always indicates the dress for the evening from casual to "formal." Speaking for myself, I must say that one of the aspects of cruise life I most appreciate is being with people who consistently care about appearance. There aren't many sloppy dressers, and I'm enough of a snob to like that.

Small-ship Cruises

Cruises don't have to be halfway to the other end of the world aboard gigantic ships weighing thousands of tons. Every bit as pleasing to the cruise-minded traveler are the small-ship tours of the Chesapeake Bay or the St. Lawrence Seaway. The American-Canadian Line offers "informal yacht-style cruise ships" to the lesser-known islands in the Caribbean, or to Canada via the Erie Canal. They also have intracoastal cruises from Rhode Island to Florida.

On the Chesapeake, there are more varied ports to visit than in any portion of the Caribbean, and a week is scarcely long enough. The *American Eagle* and the *Independence* carry 80 or 90 passengers and are as informal as might be expected. We were there in May when the softshell crabs were in season. What a treat that was. One of the best recollections of that trip for me is the fun I had reading *Beautiful Swimmers* by William W. Warner. The book's explanation of crabbing made the activities around us more understandable. The eastern shore of Maryland is gorgeous, and the prerevolutionary homes are outstanding, but the whole panorama must be seen from the water to be appreciated best.

Cruises are also available on the Mississippi River. The venerable *Delta Queen* and her younger sister, the *Mississippi Queen*, still charm passengers all the way from St. Paul to New Orleans. The *Queens* schedule cruises of varying lengths, from three days to two weeks. Four or five days is enough to get the real flavor. The *Delta Queen* is the one I know. You'd probably love her. Perfectly polished brass, gleaming mahogany and teakwood paneling, fine service featuring great southern food, a real calliope making circus music when we get into port, antebellum mansions along the shores down South and that big red paddlewheel churning along at the stern—what more could any traveler ask? "Huck Finn, eat your heart out," you'll say.

This is old-time river boating. Several years ago some of our party missed the boat (literally) in Memphis and were taken in a pickup truck to Helena, Arkansas, to get aboard. Not bothering to tie to a real dock there, the captain just brought the old queen close to the banks of the river, and four well-dressed, red-faced ladies walked a plank through the mud to our ship. At Natchez we "docked" by tying the *Delta Queen* to three trees. And so it goes. Whenever the going gets sticky, the man at the ragtime piano plays "Bye, Bye Blackbird," everybody sings along and Mississippi life is revived.

Linblad is a name long associated with the small-ship side of the cruise business. Lars-Eric Linblad has devoted his life to taking folks into far-away places, hard to get to even in today's world. Linblad often uses smaller ships like those on the Chesapeake, and adds to the personal involvement of his passengers by providing Zodiacs, those inflatable boats that Jacques Cousteau uses, to carry ten or twelve people at a time into the nooks and crannies of the world.

In my short-lived career as a cruise organizer, I had the great pleasure of a Linblad cruise in his home country, Sweden. Actually, we sailed from Helsinki across the Swedish archipelago to Stockholm. Aboard *Polaris* everyone was involved in the day's activities. In one port, one of the crew invited everyone to his grandmother's house for coffee and cakes. Mr. Linblad himself did the food shopping along the way, finding some choice tiny crabs—a real delicacy. I never knew there was so much salmon or so many varieties of herring in my life. That's a fine kind of cruising.

Smaller ships, which can make their way into ports not accessible to the big ships, are more and more popular. Names such as *World Discoverer* and *Explorer Starship* are attracting the attention of the travel editors and agents. Clipper Cruise Line's *Yorktown Clipper*, carrying only 138 passengers, will soon be cruising the waterways of the eastern seaboard, which should appeal to a lot of us who don't feel a need to journey thousands of miles from home.

Emboldened by the incredible popularity of the *Sea Cloud* (the largest sailing yacht in the world—once owned by Marjorie Meriwether Post and now generally charted by the Smithsonian, National Trust and other organizations for special voyages), sailing yacht/ships have been popping up like the Loch Ness monster around the world, particularly in the Caribbean. If you're intrigued by sailing ships, just mention *Wind Star* or *Wind Song* to your travel agent. These yachts have computer-controlled sails and plush cabins. That doesn't sound like bargain-counter travel to me. How about you?

The Cruise for You

Now—once you've decided you want to take a cruise, where do you intend to go? Where *can* you go? Almost anywhere in the world is the answer to that—although only in the Caribbean is there cruising year-round. Otherwise, ships move from the Inside Passage to Alaska or the North Cape of Norway to the South Pacific and the Indian Ocean or the Mediterranean according to the seasons. Choosing the itinerary most appealing is part of the fun of planning.

Incidentally, when considering a cruise in any direction, pay attention to the amount of time spent in the ports along the way. If most of the stops are just a few hours, that's a bad sign; nothing much to see in those places. No ships ever stay long at Gibraltar, for example. Waste of time. There will be full days in the best ports, maybe even overnight.

In port, a big decision is to join a shore excursion or explore on your own. The *Nieuw Amsterdam* (Holland America Line) makes the decision much easier. Details of the shore excursions offered are explained several times on the in-room TV sets. My old friend, Kitty, and I appreciated that. We could talk the whole thing over, then watch the film again if we were still unsure about which tour we wanted, if any.

Taking a cab or hiring a sightseeing car from the dock can be a great way to spend a day in the right port. Of course this depends on how punctual your companions are and that all-important agreement on the money and the time spent shopping before hiring the car. An English-speaking driver or guide is generally available, but test the English before driving down the road half a mile and discovering that *he or she* might call it English, but it's Greek to the rest of you.

Two well-meaning ladies on a Royal Viking cruise with me decided to leave the bus in order to spend extra minutes trying on blouses in Santo Domingo. I was dumb enough to agree to the plan, and we nearly missed the ship. Cabs were impossible to find. Plenty of men on the streets wanted to sell us lottery tickets, but nobody understood "taxi." After almost an hour of this mess, the ladies were frantic. I pretended to be calm, but when the only driver who showed up delivered the three of us to the gate of a naval base with armed guards all around, I was speechless. The guy understood "pier" and here we were. Beatrice had a postcard picture of our ship, showed it to the poor, befuddled man, and he took us straight to the correct dock just in time to race up the gangway. At least six lessons for cruise travelers must be evident in this story.

More productive shore excursions in my recent travels have included a ride on a 118-year-old train in Costa Rica, and hiring an enterprising young driver in Auckland who made and served tea from the back of his van, then spread a delightful luncheon table under the trees while we admired the New Zealand countryside.

I opted for hiring a car in the South Pacific when we docked at Vanuatu—an island we knew as New Hebrides back in the forties. That's where I met Rodger. I have a gut feeling I was not the first older woman alone who had hired Rodger's car for an hour or two of sight-seeing. Rodger and I inspected all of the palm trees, beaches and banana plantations, visited every one of his cousins' souvenir shops on this small island, looked at both "luxury" hotels, and wound up touring out into the country so I could admire the beautiful rain forests and two vacant lots which Rodger and his brother just happened to have for sale. Being excellent carpenters, they would be glad to build me a nice little vacation house which they would manage as an income property for me. I hated to tell Rodger he was nuts for thinking I could afford a home in paradise so I said he'd have to contact my son, the accountant, and gave him Chris's address.

At Suva, on Fiji, I enlisted Bobby, a local driver, to take me to the Cultural Center at Pacific Harbor—a marvelous reconstruction of Fijian traditional lifestyle. Bobby was not in the vacant lot business. He wanted to move to San Diego. "WHY?" I asked. "You live here where anything will grow, the beaches and trees and flowers are breath-taking. You live among people who appear to value their heritage. And certainly the future of the world now lies in the Pacific."

"The money's better in San Diego, and my kids could have a better education and a better life."

Bobby made a point of driving me past a cemetery where some graves were wildly decorated with flowers and festoons of palms. "This is where our soldiers are buried who have died in Beirut. The Americans saved our necks in World War II, so when you needed help with the peace-keeping forces in Lebanon, we sent Fiji troops. We haven't forgotten."

I won't forget Bobby either.

In Port Kelang, Malaysia, I insisted on buying kites, even though the kites so famous to the area were out of season. The driver of our broken-down tour car finally produced two bedraggled kites, which I still think he stole from his children.

So much for shore excursions. Seeing something new and different is one big reason for taking the trip, so enjoy.

Considering all the astonishing amounts and varieties of food, the nightclub shows, casinos, midnight buffets, dancing lessons, on-board golf lessons, bingo games, masquerade parties, exercise classes, enrichment lectures and the rest—the lavish offerings of cruise life—what is the one ingredient that makes for a really good trip? The people.

There is something unbeatable about stepping out on that deck in early morning air with a fine salty breeze, greeting other walkers grinning and groaning with dogged determination to overcome the effects of three deserts a day and survive to order another Grand Marnier soufflé. The same smiling faces show up in the theater, the lounges, the shops, the sauna, the dance floor and the beauty shop until the realization hits: these are new friends.

"Now, let's keep in touch. When you and Louise get back to Topeka, be sure to look up that guy I mentioned. And next time you're in Laguna, you'll know where to find us."

"It's been great. Let's try to travel together again next spring. How about Alaska or New England?"

And they mean it. Nice folks.

Life Is Eating and Sleeping

RESTAURANTS

Norwegian salmon with *blinis* and herb butter
Cannelonis celeri with truffle sauce
Grapefruit sorbet to cleanse the palate
Sole with artichoke and curry covered with bean thread
Dessert symphony: poached pear with *cassis* and raspberries
Crème brulée with finest slivers of orange peel

Sound good? It certainly should. That's what my friend Arthur and I had for lunch one day. Not an ordinary lunch by my standards, however. This was luncheon served at Taillevant, the four-star restaurant known among gourmets all over the world as the finest restaurant in Paris. A reservation at Taillevant is as hard to come by as a personal audience with the pope, maybe even more difficult. Arthur had struggled, waited, begged and prayed for Taillevant to grant him a reservation for luncheon for at least five years. When that big event finally occurred, he invited me to join him in Paris for lunch. Believe me, it was worth the trip.

For me to write about eating and restaurants is not much different from Mark Twain writing about the Mississippi. It's love. Appreciation of good food is one of my primary skills, perhaps the foremost one. Great meals and travel make an ideal combination in my opinion. Naturally, a meal such as that fancy luncheon in the loveliest of dining rooms with the most thoughtful service is not something to be enjoyed every day. That was once in a lifetime. But thank heaven the world is filled with good places to eat, and sampling food wherever we go is part of learning more from our travels, whether we go 20 miles or 2,000.

Before moving on from Taillevant, let's explore what makes such a fine restaurant so expensive yet worth the money to anyone truly delighted by the finest of foods. The French worship their cuisine and the master chefs, who are virtually national heros. In this particularly legendary establishment only one seating is served at luncheon or dinner. That's about 100 customers. In the kitchen are at least 16 chefs, giving undivided attention to the preparation of the freshest of meats and vegetables, the finest of sauces and so forth. A plate of lamb with mustard sauce served from that kitchen is not just lunch, it's a creation worthy of being signed by the artist. You feel sad messing it up with your fork.

All over the world there is delicious food. My travel notebooks bulge with scribbles about great meals from Denver or Taos or Saratoga Springs or Kansas City to Athens or Shanghai or Tokyo, and not necessarily in reputed restaurants winning high praise from guidebooks or critics. Many fine meals have come my way by chance or just because the menu looked interesting and the place smelled right. Number one restaurant rule: If the smell isn't right, leave.

Most of us who like to cook are interested in the preparation and variety of foods in localities beyond our own. As a matter of fact, those Time-Life cookbooks centered on faraway places are fine tour guides, well illustrated and with explicit descriptions of eating habits (and therefore lifestyles) of the countries featured.

Before traveling very far, study the cookbooks, particularly the illustrated ones, of the places you intend to visit. You'll be astonished about what help that can be when you face a menu in a foreign land. It might even be a good idea to make a note of the names of dishes you find appealing to refer to along your way. Then at least you'll know what to expect and can look forward to regional foods. I do have a handy, compact book, *The Marling Menu-Master for France*, small enough to fit into any pocket or purse. The book is divided into appetizers, soups, eggs, vegetables, meats, etc., with definitions and descriptions of specific dishes. In the back of the book is a practice menu. Similar references must be available for other countries.

Certainly, eating one's way around the world is not priority number one with most travelers. Only a few of us compare the thrill of a pail of steamed mussels in Belgium to the wonder of seeing a hit Broadway show or being on hand to watch the Broncos when they finally win the Super Bowl. But the search for outstanding food can be every bit as much a purpose for travel—and as rewarding as an archaeological dig or sighting 400 rare birds in one week.

Earlier I mentioned a great book about roadside food, featuring diners and good solid American favorites. Other reading can provide tips for good eating. Guidebooks from American Express or the *Access* series offer reliable ratings of restaurants. After all, when you're in a big city and you're pretty sure any dinner will be a major expense, why not take the advice of someone who's eaten there already? They'll point out the rip-offs too. One seafood house in New York was described very well by the reviewer who said, "The catch of the day will probably be you."

Seasoned European travelers swear by the almighty *Guide Michelin*. This is the bible of French dining-out. A three-star restaurant has passed more tests, undergone more examinations and surpassed more competitors than a Rhodes scholar. Some travel magazines have been critical of the Michelin rating of hotels lately, but when it comes to goose liver and strange mushrooms, Michelin has the final word.

Other ways to choose where to dine in unfamiliar territory? Ask friends who have been there, if their tastes are similar to your own. Get ahold of local newspapers for restaurant reviews, particularly in large cities. Read the regional tour guides available in your bookstore. Bartenders or service station attendants can be of some help occasionally. In a small town, just ride around until you spot the eatery with the most cars or a sign that announces the meeting days for civic clubs. Those people generally have sense enough to choose the best food in town when they'll be faced with it every Thursday from now until Doomsday.

I've been told that in any town of size, it's wise to shy away from an ethnic restaurant if it's the only one offering that cuisine in the area. That makes sense. If there's only one Hungarian or Moroccan restaurant in the whole town, their source of specialty supplies and suitable foodstuffs is limited. Maybe lots of passable chicken chow mein goes over the counter under such circumstances, but very little fresh veal *paprikash*.

Once driving through Columbus, Ohio, my sisters and I noticed in the AAA tour guide that a large German settlement in Columbus was quite close to our interstate. There we enjoyed one of the best Sunday dinners we've ever had. Didn't take any longer than leaving the highway for an ordinary chain restaurant either. So there's another answer to finding good food along the way: take advantage of the background and culture of each community when you can.

Getting back to my notebooks, I find rave notices (from myself) about a tiny café in the south of France where Professor Rikhoff had the best chicken of her life and my brochette of sausages and tomatoes was excellent. South of Lyon, we enjoyed trout with tomato butter and white asparagus with a special sauce. Cold steamed spinach served with oil and lemon was good enough to underline in a small taverna in Rome. And at the famous Harry's Bar in Venice, the paper-thin raw beef (*carpaccio*) was good enough to rave about the rest of my life. Most of our meals in Greece had stuffed vine leaves, eggplant in one form or another and delicious lamb. At a place in Athens called Socrates Prison, the zucchini in cream sauce with bacon and cheese certainly got our attention and the swordfish souvlaki was superb.

I think mainland Chinese food is good, but it takes a little getting used to. Sandy and I were together in China when the passengers of the *Royal Viking Star* were invited to dinner at the Great Hall of the People. This was one of those 14-course banquets, but not as elaborate as we had been served in some of the hotels. The People are not supposed to indulge in too many luxuries, but the food was undoubtedly far more typical of the daily fare of the People than that usually reserved for tourists. Nevertheless, we ate the webs of ducks' feet and lots of steamed cabbage. The *dim sum* (steamed dumplings) are good all over China.

In my opinion, the greatest contrast to that banquet in the Far East was the street food in Singapore. Singapore is such a clean city that the street food is perfectly safe and delicious. Meats cooked on skewers, beautiful fresh fruits. It's wonderful.

If asked which American restaurant I'd hurry back to, I'd have to say the choices are so wide, there's no way to pick one. We have so many good eating styles and such a variety around us. I'd be up on a stump—although in the running are Gustaf Anders in La Jolla, The Elms in Saratoga Springs, the Grist Mill on the Hudson in Warrensburg, New York, Santacafe in Santa Fe, L'Orangerie in Los Angeles, the Crab Cooker in Newport Beach, Rattlesnake Club in Denver and Beaujolais in Fort Lauderdale. I suppose the list is as boundless as my appetite.

Anyone the least bit interested in food or regional lifestyle should make a point of visiting the local markets, whether farm or city. You must get there early in the morning to see all the action—but so much vitality! In Baltimore and Philadelphia there are displays of seafood and produce that take your breath away. (The oysters served at the market in Baltimore are the best I've ever eaten—anywhere in the world.) In China there are live ducks and geese in baskets. In Japan the raw fish is astounding. In Venice you can watch the merchants and restaurateurs load mountains of fresh food into their gondolas. And of course there's always the Farmer's Market in Los Angeles.

Life is one meal after another. Being prepared and being aware of options and opportunities is every bit as important in planning and enjoying food along the way as sightseeing, hotels or beaches. Enjoy!

HOTELS

The other half of life is sleeping. Finding a good hotel makes a trip so much more pleasant. Reliable hotel reviews abound in newspapers. Travel magazines and the magazines aimed at "the good life," such as *Connoisseur*, will point out the particularly good places to stay around the world. Often the articles about the out-of-the-way bargains are most useful, particularly since so many hotel rates have soared above $100 across the country.

Here are some of my favorite hotels, each of which I present based on my own experience only.

The *Broadmoor* of Colorado Springs. Naturally. No better hotel, more beautiful setting, more fastidious decor and maintenance can be found anywhere. I mean that. The ducks on the lake, the setting at the foot of Cheyenne Mountain, the perfectly manicured golf courses, the elegant and casual dining rooms serving fine food, the shops (Papagallo, Mark Cross and their ilk, along with Broadmoor-based specialty shops), simply the feeling of walking into the place—it all adds up to a superb hotel.

The *Sagamore* at Bolton Landing on Lake George. Restoration of this century-old hotel has brought elegance back to the "Queen of American Lakes." Now operated by Omni Hotels, the Sagamore offers every amenity, including a dinner cruise on the water. The spa, condominiums, dining rooms, particularly the Sunday brunch accompanied by the finest harpsichord music, the spectacular lawn sloping to the water's edge, the "Gone-with-the-Wind" landscaping—it's all there, folks, and it's classy.

The *Inn* at *Quechee Gorge* is a prerevolutionary farmhouse just outside Quechee, Vermont, which is worth the trip—no matter how far you travel. The rooms are authentically furnished. The reception-sitting room filled with wing chairs and leather couches and footstools seems almost a time-warp place. Fine fresh-baked breakfast breads linger in my memory. This is a hotel to savor, not just a place to sleep.

The *Marriott* at *Long Wharf* in Boston is high on my list for several reasons, not the least of which is being right on the water and within walking distance of Quincy Market and the rest of the Freedom Trail. The atmosphere and decor are outstanding and the food is better than in most hotels.

The *Red Lion Inn* at Stockbridge, Massachusetts, ranks as a real favorite. This is a step back in time, but more enjoyable if you manage to avoid peak-of-the-season crowds. Right on Main Street, close to fancy shops and old-fashioned stores, the Red Lion is just steps away from the Norman Rockwell Museum. Norman Rockwell must have enjoyed rocking on the porch of the Red Lion Inn, or relishing the fine food in the gracious dining room.

The *Peabody Hotel* at *Orlando*, younger sister of the venerable Peabody of Memphis, is a treat. There's no doubt about that. The interior decor is largely white marble, the gigantic bouquets are sprays of orchids, the pools and grounds are a delight to the eye, even the red-carpet parade of ducks through the lobby is wondrous. Particularly to be recommended is the carpaccio (raw beef) served in the Italian restaurant, Capriccio. This hotel has the uncanny knack of making guests feel well cared for even at a convention. That's something!

The *Stanford Court* in San Francisco and the *Huntington* are my choices because they epitomize old San Francisco. The courtyard entry to the Stanford Court must have been intended for carriages. The view from most rooms is splendid.

The *Carlyle* boasts the only five-star rating in New York City. I'll take that back: the Carlyle is too well mannered to *boast* about anything. The Carlyle assumes we know about the five stars. Until the rates went out of (my) sight, I stayed there regularly because of the elegance, the personal approach to service—I honestly was their *guest*. And because Bobby Short entertained nightly in the Café Carlyle, and a lady could listen alone without feeling awkward. New York is a walking city, of course, and the Carlyle is well situated for walking to either the Metropolitan Museum of Art or the shopping on Fifth Avenue. (Incidentally, the Carlyle still has elevator operators. For women traveling alone, I find it's remarkable how much better it feels to know there is personal service provided, even in the elevators. That's real security.)

The *Willard* in Washington, D.C. Here's another restoration of a grand old place. The Willard was boarded up, a complete shambles inside, when some wonderful soul invested millions of dollars to bring back one of the gems of Washington. The Willard is superb, far more than the Mayflower or other traditions of Washington hostelry. Just the ceiling of the lobby, seals of every state in gilt and brilliant colors, makes the Willard worth a visit. My own criterion for "class" is ceilings. (Notice the elegance overhead in the Broadmoor, for example. Wonderful.)

The *Capital Holiday Inn* in Washington, D.C. For family-oriented visits to Washington, none can compare with this Holiday Inn just behind the Museum of Air and Space. All of the Mall is at hand. This is convenient, well run and affordable. Take the family to the Holiday Inn; basking at the Willard is for travel without the children.

Rancho Encantado in Santa Fe. I feel almost disloyal to the La Fonda (where we honeymooned 43 years ago), but this is *the* place for Santa Fe as far as elegance and comfort, combined with traditional architecture and the Spirit of Santa Fe, are concerned. The Santa Fe Opera is just down the road.

L'Auberge of Sedona, located in this most charming of Arizona haunts, is a combination of log cabins beside Oak Creek, a regular hotel, and the finest Provençal restaurant west of St. Tropez. It all adds up to perfection.

Enchantment near Sedona, Arizona. This is John Gardner's tennis ranch, a spectacular example of fitting the architecture of the Southwest into a canyon of unparalleled beauty and grandeur. If I sound overwhelmed, it's because I am. This is not glitzy in any sense. Quality shines here. I'll never be a tennis player, but I'd love to try to look like one at Enchantment.

Graham's Bed and Breakfast, also in Sedona, is the only bed and breakfast I've experienced that has a four-star rating from the Mobil guide. The Grahams, Bill and Marnie, deserve every one of those stars and more. Their accommodations are more like suites, the atmosphere relaxed and comfortable, the breakfast unusual, and the overall stay with the Grahams is a joy.

Remarkable in the hotel world are these even more exotic places to stay.

The *Mandarin* in Hong Kong, with her sister hotel, the *Oriental* in Bangkok, are proclaimed to be the finest hotels in the world by many authorities. Not everyone agrees, of course; after all, the whole world is a mighty big place with a wide choice of fine hotels. But having stayed in both of these with great joy and satisfaction, I will say I have never seen any setting lovelier anywhere, anytime, than the pool at the Mandarin. That pool typifies the entire establishment. Absolute serene beauty. The Regent and the Peninsula are fine Hong Kong hotels, but I'll take the Mandarin every time.

My travel-agent boss, Judy Smith, and I marveled at our room in the Oriental when in Bangkok. This was no sumptuous suite, but the arrangement of closets, luggage space, and the size and workability of the bathroom were outstanding. There was a quality there hard to identify but very real.

The *Intercontinental Hotel*, built into the old Treasury Building in Sydney, is a marvel of architectural engineering and great decor. Service was exemplary when I was there and all state-of-the-art. For example, whenever I picked up my phone to ask for anything—even a wake up call—the operator said, "May I help you, Mrs. Weaver?" I spent hours wondering how he recognized my voice, then figured out that each guest's name is flashed on the computer screen as the phone rings. Isn't that fine? We all love hearing our own name, especially half a world away from home.

The old *Peking Hotel* in Beijing belongs on my great hotel list because it was old and relatively unchanged when Judy Smith and I were there in 1981. Faded velvet draperies, inkwells in the desks—all had been new before 1910, and were still in place. Now Americans are generally housed at the Great Wall Hotel, a Sheraton, which is no different from staying in downtown Dallas.

The flavor of "real" China survived in the unwesternized *Peace Hotel* in Shanghai at least until 1981, when I stayed there: vintage furnishings from the days just before I was born. You should have seen the permanent-wave machines in the barber shop on the mezzanine. Probably that hotel has been updated now, too. The Chinese realize the penchant of American visitors for having everything "just like home." More's the pity.

Back on this side of the world for my first choice, however. The *Indianapolis Holiday Inn* crowns my hotel list. Downtown Indianapolis has undergone an astonishing facelift in recent years, and the jewel is the Holiday Inn created in connection with the aristocratic Union Station. I couldn't believe it. The hotel is constructed around the old train platforms, girders still in place. My room was in a Pullman car, and it was lovely. Best of all, beside the basic ingenuity of design, is the artwork. George Segal–sculptured, white figures are all over the place. Beside the train-car steps to my room stood a stark, white sailor with his seabag, waiting for the next train to San Diego, I suppose.

This Holiday Inn is not only a charming place to stay; it's a fine example of a city with sense enough to preserve what is good and beautiful of its past for use in today's world. Congratulations, Holiday Inn and Indianapolis.

When choosing your hotel, remember any chain or group of hotels will happily provide a booklet listing all of their locations. And one Best Western, for example, will be happy to help you find accommodations in the next one down your road. Also, 800 numbers are convenient for reserving rooms with Hilton,

Sheraton and other chains. Just call directory assistance 1-800-555-1212 for reservation numbers. I usually make hotel reservations on my own; travel agents can do it, but direct contact pleases me for some reason, and I can always ask for a senior citizen's discount. Don't forget that part—Sheraton, for example, offers 25 percent off to anyone over 60. One more advantage to these Golden Years.

How Long Will It Take You to Get Ready?

Sally Council has one of those nifty fold-up plastic carriers for toiletries and such. She showed it to me when we first met as "Smithsonian Students" at Oxford; then last summer she showed up carrying the same handy gadget for a two-day jaunt to Tanglewood to hear the Boston Symphony.

There must be a dozen pockets of varying sizes in this plastic masterpiece. All are zippable. It's a good-looking and astonishingly easy-to-pack convenience. Sally never unpacks it. When she gets home from a trip, whether it's been for a weekend or a month, she replaces any used-up items and puts the whole kit and caboodle in the "travel drawer" in her bathroom.

THIS YEAR I PLAN TO GO ELSEWHERE

Now Sally hasn't confined her stock of travel items to the expected necessities like toothbrush and combs. Tucked in those see-through pockets are a sewing kit from some long-forgotten Holiday Inn, a tube of Woolite, extra batteries for Sally's camera, a magic marker just in case; all sorts of things. The makeup base is a neutral shade. Eye makeup and blush she bought in small sizes as a bonus purchase of Estee Lauder. Same for the lotion and shampoo. Extra tweezers, razor, nail clippers and files are packed in, all in order.

Until she discovered this gem of travel readiness, Sally claims she wasted untold hours fussing about what to include in her little makeup satchel. Almost everything she put in there was spilled or messed up. Some vital item for Sally's *toilet* was always missing. She wasted vacation time buying deodorant. Now even her vitamin pills, calcium tablets and hormone capsules are at the ready because an additional supply is packed. Here comes the neatest part: when she checks into a hotel or arrives in my guest room, that little dandy hangs on a hook in the bathroom with all of those supplies in plain sight. Whether she has traveled overnight or overseas, Sally is prepared—she's even included band-aids and extra film.

Traveling businessmen have practiced this sort of pre-paredness as a matter of course. But it's news to women like me who have taken travel as a special event in our lives rather than as a regular occurrence. We have sense enough to keep an old coat and a pair of snow boots in the trunk of the car year-round. Being ready to take off at a moment's notice is no different, just a trifle more exotic.

Not to be overlooked is the message we receive about Sally's state of mind. Not only is Sally's toothbrush on standby, so is this sixtyish woman. No event or opportunity for expanding horizons is too big or too small for Sally's consideration— around the block or across the state. You'd like Sally. She's one of my "travel bonuses." Since we first met while both traveling alone with the Smithsonian group, I've learned a lot from this most enthusiastic friend—only I keep *my* cosmetic case in the linen closet.

HOW LONG WILL IT TAKE YOU TO GET READY?

All of us can be organized enough to leave home on short notice should the temptation arise to visit the grandchildren or explore the Glassworks Museum at Corning, New York, or flirt with Lady Luck in Las Vegas or Atlantic City. It's akin to having a head start, and that's smart.

Take the same approach to basic clothes when packing. It will make life simpler if you keep the essentials in a carry-on bag—a nightie, a robe of some sort, a pair or two of pantyhose, and anything else you have an extra set of. Just put this half-packed traveling case in the guestroom closet. Then fix another for your husband. When the time comes, add a clean shirt and trousers or whatever and be off. Just like that.

The same sort of planning works well with the car. At least it does for me. Having left my atlas on the kitchen counter three trips in a row, I now keep it in the pocket on the door of the passenger side. There's a minimal first-aid kit in the glove compartment, along with the AAA manuals and emergency phone numbers. Never take them out.

In addition to having your toiletries and overnight bag prepared and your glove compartment stocked, there is some paperwork that should be ready. Keep photocopies of your tickets, credit cards, driver's license, passport, travelers check records and the like in your overnight bag (and separate copies in a safe place at home). Often, you are asked for your passport number. To have the photocopy eliminates having to fish for the passport itself, thereby running the risk of forgetting or losing it. Pack the copies of check records and such in separate luggage, *not* in that overburdened wallet or purse.

My next suggestion sounds simplistic, but it counts so much. Don't ever be caught without a workable, attractive idea about someplace to go. When the old boredom conversation starts all over again in your crowd, be the first to say, "Why don't we get away for a while?" Then, have a definite proposal to offer. "Have you seen the special exhibition at the Natural History Museum in Denver?" would be a logical opening for such a project here in Colorado. Wherever you live, there is something of interest, something different, within half-a-day's drive—but you and your family, spouse or friends will overlook such opportunities if you're not tuned in to collecting getaway ideas. The best approach is to make a habit of reading the big-city newspapers, particularly the Sunday papers or often the Thursday or Friday "Weekend" sections. There is a treasure trove of attractions and events in the Denver area, for example, or in the Colorado Springs region, which people in my part of Colorado can enjoy if we take the time to find out about what's going on.

Picture yourself in an encounter like this. Say you're at the supermarket and your old friend Grace comes around the corner from behind a Fritos display.

"Grace! It's been months since I've seen you. How's everything?"

"Okay, I guess. I'm sick of this weather and the same old stuff. Haven't heard from the kids for more than a week, and my arthritis is acting up again. All I seem to get done these days is. . . ."

Now it's your turn. You tell her about your backaches or how lonely it is at your house. You say, "Well, Grace, let's get together and have lunch some day next week. We have so much to talk about."

Face it, in your heart you know you have nothing to talk about except complaints. Or you could be tempted to issue another vague invitation like, "I'd love to get away for a day or two."

She might say, "That sounds great. Where would you like to go?"

You might stammer, "Oh, surely we can think of something. . . . I'll call you."

Then she goes back to worrying about her arthritis and you go back to moaning about your bad back. Nonsense, isn't it? Two adult women with nothing to do but gripe.

Let's re-run the conversation:

"Grace! It's been months! How's everything?"

"Okay, I guess, I'm sick of this weather. . . ."

Don't let her finish. She'll just feel worse. "I'm sick of it, too. I've decided I'd like to explore that new French department

82

store in Denver and maybe the new Italian hotel near Cherry Creek. How about going up one day next week? We can stay overnight. Really live it up."

"What a good idea. My neighbor can take care of my dog, I guess. Let me check it out, because I'd love doing something different. Maybe Lois would like to. . . . I'll call her. And how about Sandy? We could have a bridge game in the hotel room. I'll call you as soon as. . . . "

And off you both go, feeling better about the whole world. That will not happen unless we are alert enough to have an impromptu excursion in mind. Here's one of my tentative plans to suggest to a friend; it might give you some leads in your own part of the world. (I'm just waiting for the right time to use it.) I am not a skier—never have been. One day I'd love to drive to Vail or Aspen or some glamorous ski spot just to watch what goes on, sample the restaurants, and hear what my skiing friends and family are talking about. The same can be true of going out to observe hot-air balloons or hang glider enthusiasts or bird watchers. Expand horizons and understanding and take a day or two away from the routine, the expected in life. If you're ready, it's there for you.

Let's get back to Grace and her dog for a minute: keep your place ready to leave. Home responsibilities can hold many would-be vagabonds in their houses with grass to mow, plants to water, pets to feed, snow to shovel or dead blossoms to pick off the geraniums.

Here we need to stop and reassess our priorities. Personally, I gave up on geraniums long ago in favor of being able to shut the door on a moment's notice and take off in pursuit of some new adventure. There has never been a period when so many of us have such free time and so many options at any age. Gone from my life are the days when I read enticing accounts of craft shows or white-water rafting races or opening of new plays and resented the fact that I had no time for such things in a busy, young, family-filled life. Now those days may be gone from your life too.

We all need to be needed. That's one reason for having a dog. But we also must be responsible for our own emotional well-being, and a ferry ride to Vermont or a midweek stay at Lake Tahoe might do more for us than tying ourselves to the house with another mouth to feed—even if the fare is Kal Kan. A think-ahead plan involving a neighbor to see to house and pet care is vital, so we can be at the ready when the chance to take off for a while comes into our lives. We're not talking about a lengthy trip to China here—just a day or two of "R and R" as the Army calls it.

Think ahead about the small chores of everyday life that might get in your way if you decide to leave home without full-scale deck-clearing. It's astonishing how much we put off day to day. Don't let the bills pile up until you are in a mood to part with all that money; pay them as they arrive every day or two, then you won't stay up past your bedtime messing with the paperwork at the last minute. In other words, keep your life up-to-date, to avoid a frenetic rush to set things in order on short notice. If you make too much trouble for yourself preparing to leave town, you can spoil a good time before you ever shut the overnight case and leave a note for the paper carrier.

The Boy Scouts figured it out years ago: be prepared. Do a little Scoutwork on your own behalf. Otherwise, Sally will fold up her cosmetics case, I'll hop in my car to pick up Grace and Lois, and you'll be left sitting there fussing about your dentist appointment and why your kids haven't called since Sunday.

"There's This Neat Place I Read About..."

Travel books—there must be thousands of them, ever since the *Odyssey*. Encouraged by the increase in tourism into the nooks and crannies of the world, from southern Utah to the Great Wall, the publishing industry has gone a little crazy about guide books. Every city, park or hiking trail west of any given point is mapped, described and evaluated in every form, ranging from $3.95 paperbacks about nature study in the Ozarks to $40 encyclopedias of British country gardens.

This is fine and good fun and a boon to aspiring travel writers the world over. But how do we make a choice? How can we decide which of those full-color, beautifully illustrated volumes is best for the trip we are planning? Which is the most usable, most practical, most exotic or most reliable guide book to study beforehand and to tote along?

Your best choice depends upon: (1) what sort of advice you are seeking, and (2) how and where your journeys will take you.

Let's start with long-range planning for extensive travel. What used to be called the Grand Tour of Europe is old hat these days, but, for the vast majority of us, a trip to Europe or the Far East or a two-week cruise through the Panama Canal is a once-in-a-lifetime event. We don't want to shortchange ourselves.

Before investing time or money in books, make an effort to talk to someone who has been there. Wherever "there" might be.

What were their good and bad experiences?

What did they overlook or particularly enjoy?

How about language and money-changing problems?

Which guide books worked best for them?

What sort of clothes worked best?

Should you be wary of drinking water and such?

How about public transportation?

Which restaurants and food were their favorites?

Most important: What would they do differently on a return trip?

Before John and I made our one and only trip to Hawaii, we cornered our neighbors and friends who were Hawaii buffs and asked one question: "If you returned to Hawaii, to stay on only one island, which would you choose?" Unanimous response was "Maui," which simplified our planning and was excellent advice.

Of course, when asking these questions, consider the source of the answer. If your crabby cousin has nothing good to say about St. Thomas or Barbados, ask somebody else. Your cousin probably wouldn't like *any* place in her present frame of mind.

After gleaning whatever you can from firsthand accounts, start reading. Travel magazines like *Travel and Leisure* and *Traveler*, Conde Nast's travel monthly, can point you in the right direction for the most current details. The restaurant reviews, hotel evaluations and special-event reportage are excellent as well as enticing. The same holds true for newspaper travel sections, but don't rely on them for too long—keep up with change. From this preliminary study, you will find yourself focusing on your own special interests for this trip. Maybe food, maybe music, perhaps archaeology or local history. Who knows?

Then you're ready to plow through the hundreds of books on the travel-section shelves and leaf through the ones most appealing. You will find material geared for all sorts and conditions of folks: budget travelers, culture vultures, campers and backpackers, RVers, sailing enthusiasts and all the rest.

Discrimination is the key here. Rule number one: Do not buy too many books. In some cases, two is too many. Remember, if you want to carry these along with you, dragging around ten pounds of reference books is dumb.

In 1983 my friend the professor and I sat cross-legged on the floor in a sea of newspaper tear sheets, magazine articles and guide books for one entire winter planning our upcoming two-month odyssey through Greece, Italy and France. I finally got bored with this exercise and gave up, so she learned a lot more than I from the experience. Then we did the silliest thing; instead of taking useful notes, we bundled up the whole mess and hauled it with us. We had three books about every place we might possibly visit during this nomad adventure. We carried Frommer's for the cheap stuff, Fodor for the reliability we'd heard about, and miscellaneous other reading material which said basically the same thing for reasons that had blurred before we ever repacked that load for the fifth time in six days.

By the time we reached Mykonos we were completely overloaded, since along the way we had picked up local guide books better than what we already had. Nuts. We were wasting time, energy and money with too much repetitive information. Actually most useful to us in Greece was the American Express guide. This little book was easy to carry in a pocket and had walking tours, historical and architectural information.

How have I chosen which books to include in this chapter? Believe me, it's been fun. From my own shelves of travel material I have gleaned useful books from past trips. In book-stores I have examined at least two of every category or series available. I can't claim to be an expert, but this should be an adequate sampling to get you on your way.

TRAVEL GUIDES. I divide these into categories. First, personalized advice. Let's take *Going Alone* by Carol Chester. Subtitle: *The Woman's Guide to Travel Know How*. Here's a sample quote about dining alone in England: "Cafés vary. . . . Have a good look before you go in and don't be afraid of walking out again if the interior doesn't appeal." Carol Chester adds a warning: "It's well to know that hotel watering spots, in London at least, do attract high-class prostitutes and you may run the risk of being mistaken for one if you're on your own, particularly by the Middle Eastern clientele." Not many of us need that sort of precaution, but quoting it should liven up the conversation at lunch some day. The lists of "No-No's," "Essentials" and "What to Do Solo" are worth the price of the book if you are going abroad. The American section is minimal.

Personal advice travel expertise is abundant. *Places to Go with Children in Northern California* by my friend Elizabeth Pomada is representative of the wide range these books cover. Here's a fine example of how focused and specific today's travel books can get.

Means of transportation is another category. I've found specific information about cruises, walking tours, vacations in the car, canal barges, bicycle journeys, European trains, ferry-liners—and of course my new addiction, ferries.

CRUISES. Frommer's *Dollarwise Guide to Cruises* strikes me as being complete and fair in its appraisal of cruise ships and itineraries. (Don't forget that cruise ships are proliferating as fast as guppies these days, so do get the latest edition.) Certainly your travel agent has a wealth of material in the files about cruises, but be careful about the pictures in those brochures. A wide-angle lens can do wonders for a skimpy cabin. Notice the furnishings in any picture—if there's only one small chair or those grinning models are sitting on the beds, beware! What counts most to me in choosing a ship is the number of square feet per passenger listed in the most reliable cruise atlases in your agent's office. The more square footage, the better time you'll have. Numbers vary from 20 plus for the Princess or Costa lines to 50 plus for the Sagafjord.

WALKING TOURS. Walking tours are gaining popularity, at least in the publishing world. An excellent example of such a book is *Chicago on Foot: Walking Tours of Chicago's Architecture* written by Ira Bach and Susan Wolfson. Now here is my suggested procedure for choosing a walking tour guide. Scan those on the shelves in your hometown store and also check all-purpose guide books for walking-tour directions, but wait to buy your guide until you are on the spot. Example: Between trains in Chicago, I was in a cab headed for the Art Institute. "Every time I'm in Chicago, it seems some other building is being demolished or a new one is going up, " I remarked to the driver, just being friendly.

"That's right, Ma'am. We just hope they don't wreck any of our good buildings. We have some fine architecture here in Chicago. See that one on the corner there? That's a Louis Sullivan building. Of course you can tell that by the windows there. Notice the Sullivan windows over here too."

This most enlightening lecture about the buildings and architects of Chicago went on until we had stopped in front of the Art Institute.

"How do you know all that about your city?" I asked. "This has been more than a ride, it's been an education, and I appreciate it."

The driver held up a big fat book. "This here is my bible." *Chicago on Foot.*

Well, it ended up he not only picked me up in time to take me past B. Dalton, where he knew I could buy the book, but he also gave me a guided tour of the impressive public library on the way back to the station. Now that's a walking tour book I'm going to enjoy.

Samples of walking tours abound in my stack of clipped travel writing treasures. Most notable, strolling the Benjamin

Franklin Parkway in Philadelphia. This starts at City Hall and winds up in Fairmount Park with the Philadelphia Museum of Art. Any city map can point the way to such a rewarding trip. You might want to commence your own tour at 11:15 by listening to a concert played on the massive organ in the Grand Court of the John Wanamaker department store, then proceed to admire the 250 sculptures adorning City Hall. Tours of City Hall are free every day at 12:30. Philadelphia offers other exciting routes for walking which include Independence Hall too.

Los Angeles, downtown, comes highly recommended for walking tours, although most of us forget L.A. exists off the freeways. With Pershing Square as a pivotal point, it is possible to explore the compact space where pedestrians outnumber cars. That doesn't happen many places in L.A. An easy walking tour can include the Museum of Contemporary Art, the Music Center, the Bradbury Building (famous as the setting for many movies), the elegant old Biltmore Hotel, the Arco Plaza, and other landmark buildings—all in about three hours.

Walking tours in Manhattan developed by the New York Historical Society, described as "forays on foot," attract participants from all over the world who are fascinated by the city and its historic architecture. These are offered in the fall, principally, and each takes about two hours. Detailed information is certainly available from the New York Historical Society.

However, as for those "walking tours" that have been laid out by some joker from West Los Angeles out to make a fast buck inventing hikes through downtown Charleston or whatever—we don't need those.

Before we move on from walking tours I must recommend the *Access* series of guide books, which are color-coded directions for walking through the Upper East Side or wherever. Paragraphs in black are architecture, blue for hotels, red for restaurants and so on. The *Access Tokyo* guide offers another great feature: side-by-side columns are in Japanese and English, so you can stop any friendly looking person on the street, show him or her what you are trying to find written in Japanese and be understood. You probably won't understand the answer, but it will be a unique experience to share with folks at home.

90

AUTOMOBILE TRIPS. After walking tours we come to vacations by automobile, which were discussed at length in Chapter 6. Here are some of the reference works I find most useful. It would be hard to beat the AAA regional tour books. These list almost anything any of us might need to know: recreation areas, camp sites, museums, national monuments, motels, sightseeing tours, wilderness areas, restorations, scenic drives. *AAA Tour Books* alone are worth the price of AAA membership—even if that membership didn't include towing and other emergency services. American Automobile Association will also prepare for each of us a mile-by-mile itinerary for specific travel, listing side trips, lodging, roads under construction, bridges out and such. That's called a "Triptik."

Other motoring advice is specifically offered in the *Reader's Digest* volume, *Off the Beaten Path*, which lists 1,000 places that are uncrowded and inviting. After studying the portions of this publication dealing with the areas I know best, I'd say it's an excellent resource for interesting, off-the-freeways tripping. Bookstores have this one.

Roadside histories of various regions are also a good buy. I have seen the ones for Colorado and Texas. This is an offbeat way to familiarize ourselves with the territory in a "hands-on" sort of way. Very good.

Yankee magazine has published a short-trips series of books highlighting local interest and history. The one about New York State is the only one I've examined, but I have it, and use it regularly. The Saratoga Springs section is a joy.

In the Tattered Cover Bookshop in Denver, I must have seen a dozen or more books from the *Day Trip* series by Patricia and Robert Foulke, friends of mine who have glorious suggestions for day-tripping in the Middle Atlantic states and New England. I can hardly wait to get to Burlington, Vermont, to take a cruise on the *Richard Robbins*, a schooner built in 1902, or to visit the Reluctant Panther Inn in Manchester Village to experience the taste treat of the Panther Blossom—half orange juice, half cranberry juice. That's the sort of information the Foulkes provide.

A colorful set of similar, but smaller books is Shifra Stein's

Day Trips: Getaways Less Than Two Hours Away, which focuses on the areas surrounding cities such as Houston, Baltimore, Phoenix. Arranged according to direction from the central point, these are well planned and beautifully explained. Good books.

Along that same line are the bed and breakfast directories and the "country inns." This is another field that is growing very fast, so we find a variety of guide books on the shelves. Some, like Frommer's *Bed and Breakfast, North America*, are primarily source books listing reservation organizations but few individual B&B facilities. Others are ratings and listings of exactly what accommodations are available in which area. Some of these are compilations of bed and breakfast places that have paid to have their names in the book. Others are more objective assessments. The day-trip guides often include recommended B&B locations too. As with almost every other segment of travel writing, the choice is wide here.

The country inns are often historic places preserved carefully. These can be an extraordinary treat. My sisters and I stayed one night at the Black Bass Inn in New Hope, Pennsylvania, and loved every minute of it, even though we had a devil of a time finding our way there on a rainy night. We had found that jewel in a set of books published by *Architectural Digest* several years ago. Other authors particularly interested in architecture and local history have put together local directories of legendary National Trust–type inns. The books seem to be regional, so ask your bookseller.

While bookshop browsing, don't miss the *Insight Guides* group. These are state-by-state and worldwide. The photography is excellent. These look to me to be as much fun to read after the fact as during the trip. The Southwest version is particularly attractive. If I didn't live so close to New Mexico, I'd be on my way there right now because of this beauty.

Let's hear one cheer for the specialized travelers who share their enthusiasm with the rest of us. *Roadside Food*, for example, is a dandy written by LeRoy Woodson and several of his friends. This man's quest for the home-style cooking of roadside eateries of tradition is enough to make your mouth water. LeRoy and the gang have set Miss Sarah and me off on our scavenger hunt for hambugers and hot dogs that had opened up a whole new world.

I was attracted to the blue and yellow cover of *Celebrations* by Judith Young; this book lists and describes festivals and happenings all over the USA, including the International Brick and Rolling Pin Throw in Stroud, Oklahoma, and the Great American Chocolate Festival at Hershey, Pennsylvania. That's another helpful, if not downright inspirational, fund of information to be used in planning an out-of-the-ordinary getaway.

Add to these the old reliables—Frommer's, Fodor's, the American Express guides, plus those marvelous articles from travel magazines, the *National Geographic* and the *Smithsonian*, and your travel plans are a cinch. There's one catch: the more you get into these books, the more you'll want to get going.

Is This Book Done Yet?

No. This book is not done yet because a book of this kind is never finished. No writer like me can take a manuscript like this to the publisher and say, "That's that. This book is complete." Instead, you simply quit. Wrap it up. Say a few kind words to convince the reader you've done the best you can, and stop writing.

Why? Because the subject can never be closed. Since those days (which seem long ago) when I first told you about the family of my mother-in-law walking from Iowa to Kansas behind a flock of sheep, at least a thousand useful articles of travel information have been published in periodicals, brochures, pamphlets, books and ads. Some I have included, some I have ignored or set aside because there has to be a limit. Travel writing resembles cookbook production: one more fine recipe for a green-bean casserole or French onion soup manages to turn up just as the pub date seems imminent.

In the last year I have cruised through the Panama Canal and visited ports in Mexico, Columbia, Costa Rica and the Caribbean. On book business and giving speeches to women's groups, I have toured extensively in Arizona, spent time in California at least twice, also touched bases in Minnesota, Michigan, Vermont, New Hampshire, New Mexico and around my homes in Colorado and New York. Weeks have been spent in Florida. June was whiled away in the three-star restaurants and art museums of France, my vacation travel for the year. Undoubtedly I have left other trips out—almost forgot Texas.

A summary? Of course. Broken down into lists? Of course; nobody depends more on lists than I do. (Heavens, how could I have left Cleveland out of that recital in the last paragraph?)

1. TRAVEL NEED NOT BE EXPENSIVE OR EXTENSIVE to be worthwhile. Examples abound. With the old draw-around-your-hometown-with-a-jar-lid trick, any one of us can locate small museums, historic settlements, all sorts of sights.

As our children grew up, their favorite summer outing was a visit with their Weaver grandparents, who delighted in driving those kids all over Cloud County, Kansas, to see such wonders as a town called Aurora where everyone spoke French, the home of Boston Corbett (the man who shot John Wilkes Booth), and fine limestone formations literally filled with fossils of sea animals right there in north-central Kansas. I have no idea what else they saw, but those days of the back-roads with their grandparents were some of the most important learning and loving experiences of their lives.

A great Sunday outing near Houston is the Brazos State Park, where alligators sun themselves and the fish are biting. A fine overnight from any point in New York State is Corning, with its glassworks and museums, or Cooperstown, or Ticonderoga or West Point. All over America that story remains the same.

High on my 1988 collection of joys of short-tripping are the museum at Cañon City, Colorado, with arrowheads and dressed fleas, and the organ recital at Round Lake, New York, on a summer Sunday evening. Two contrasting yet similar experiences.

There's a welcome nostalgia in the treasures donated by Cañon City citizens to be displayed for the good of their community—not the stuff for which headline-making prices are paid by giant corporations at Sotheby's auctions and that will be housed or hidden in fine marble walls. Townspeople brought fans from Japan, lace from Belgium, vases from China, all carted back home from a once-in-a-lifetime trip for all of Cañon City to share. Small-town museums are like everybody's attic or everyone's basement or barn. Great Uncle's tools and Great Grandmother's kitchen are represented in their displays. There's a small-town museum or maybe even a dozen, close to you.

Perhaps an organ like the one at Round Lake can be found in your area, maybe not. My friend Philip and I went to one of the Sunday evening organ recitals at Round Lake quite by chance. We were just out roaming the countryside on a Sunday afternoon and saw the sign. Well, the organ is a wonder. It must be close to a hundred years old. I understand it has been totally rescued and rebuilt by the efforts of one woman in Round Lake. And the music was thrilling. No amplifiers or speakers, but that old organ sounded like the "mighty Wurlitzer" at Radio City Music Hall when a guest organist from St. Louis got it going. Not a big deal or an expensive outing, but Philip and I went home feeling rejuvenated ourselves, as surely as if we had indulged in an expensive weekend in some fine resort. Maybe more so. There's something equally worthwhile waiting for a visit from you in your neighborhood. Look around.

2. PURPOSE. We've talked enough about that in earlier chapters, but to my mind, the principal reason to go anyplace is to come home at least a little smarter.

3. HOMEWORK COUNTS. Unless you know about the extent of copper mining in southeast Arizona before you head in that direction, you'll miss seeing some of the most amazing, largest, most productive open pit mines in the world just a few miles off the interstate highway. If you haven't studied about

the locks and canals and ferries across our country, you are certain to overlook opportunities that could make your vacation a real winner. (Did you know you can get to the airport in Boston by ferry?) Knowing where you're going means more than reading the road map.

Two or three years ago, I read Calvin Trillin's piece in the *New Yorker* about the "Rib Burn-Off" in Cleveland. Granddaughter Jenny and I just happened to land in Cleveland on the big day of the Burn-Off this summer. Thanks to Trillin and his article, we had sense enough to realize we had lucked out, the ribs were cooking as if in honor of our trip to Cleveland. What fun. Thousands of munching folks sampling ribs from scores of barbecue booths swarmed around us as we tested ribs, drank lemonade by the gallon and dripped butter down our chins from the corn. Thanks, Mr. Trillin.

4. SIMPLIFY WHENEVER POSSIBLE, but do not cut corners. Remember those dreadful vacations when the kids were little and we tried to jam three weeks' worth of activities into one week away from home? We've all done it. Tried to visit relatives, show the children Mount Rushmore and the Grand Canyon, dragged poor old dad from one motel to the next without time for a decent nap, stopped in to see old college friends and made it through Disneyland before pulling in to the old home driveway totally exhausted and mad at each other.

Don't do that anymore. Concentrate on one vacation option. If you decide on the opera in Santa Fe, go to the opera, pure and simple. Forget trying to take in all the cliff dwellings and Indian ruins. Save those for the Indian ruins trip next year.

5. TAKE ALONG WHATEVER IS NECESSARY for your comfort, but leave convenience at home. Certainly there's no place like home. Nobody had to tell us that. The problem arises when some traveler thinks she must have all of the small conveniences of home while out on the road. Forget it. Carrying along your lighted makeup mirror and your own pillow or coffee maker only weighs down your luggage and makes room-sharing a chore.

6. BE PREPARED TO ENJOY WHATEVER YOU FIND. Look for surprises. One of my grandsons and I were at Quincy

Market in Boston, totally submerged in the expected—shops, food stalls and restaurants, souvenirs, fancy stores. Suddenly Jason stopped in his tracks, staring. "Look at this, Oma, it's a statue." There on a bronze bench was a bronze figure of a man, holding a cigar; intent, thoughtful, relaxed. Not on a pedestal above us. This statue sat there beside us. "That's Red Auerbach, the great coach of the Celtics," Jason told me. What greater thrill for a basketball-playing teenager than that? We were both close to tears at this unexpected encounter with one of Boston's Finest. That's what I mean by watch for surprises. Walking right on by could have been easy, but that moment will stand out forever for Jason and me.

In order to relive the special surprises of your trips, never overlook the value of postcards as vivid reminders of your favorite spots. By jotting a few lines about your day then mailing these cards to yourself, you'll have a ready-made travel diary when you get home. Also, those nifty double cards in bound booklets (send the card, keep the matching tab) enhance your reminiscence later, with scenery and works of art you've enjoyed in your travels. Incidentally, resist the urge to throw away those stacks of accumulated ship's newspapers, menus and programs (even the game sheets and puzzles) you've collected. You'll be sorry, since these items represent a great record of your vacation. Make sure you have an outside pocket on some carry-on just for the paperwork.

7. GRANDCHILDREN CAN BE YOUR BEST TRAVEL COMPANIONS. That little story about Jason and the statue illustrates what I want to tell you. Particularly, one or two at a time, the younger generation in your family will enjoy your attention all to themselves as much as you appreciate the opportunity to know each one better, whether for a day or two or for weeks at a time.

I was really tickled to meet Jim Newton from Florida when he was vacationing in Colorado. Two grandsons had come along, so these three guys were "batching" together and apparently having a glorious time. "Hey, wait a minute," I told him. "Traveling with grandkids is usually what grandmothers do. My dad was the only grandfather I ever knew who took grandsons on a vacation. My sons loved it when they drove all over the country with their cousins and my father. You're giving these boys a very special time to remember." Jim just grinned. "I'm having just as much fun as they are."

Think about this. Often you, the grandparent, are in a position to spend time traveling when parents cannot. Today, working couples are more the rule than the exception, and time off for both parents limits their freedom to do all they want with the children, especially older youngsters. When time comes for going to camp or looking at colleges, volunteer your services. When the kids can help with the driving, you can have a great time, a special time, before they suddenly turn into adults.

8. UNTIL YOU'VE TRIED IT, DON'T KNOCK IT. "Most folks are down on the things they aren't up on," or so said my father-in-law. We all know people who are so dead set against anything unfamiliar, they lose out on half the fun. "I never go there," or "I wouldn't be interested," or "That's just not my style," can cheat us out of travel adventures and advantages. Beware.

9. NOW IT'S OUR TURN (a special message for senior travelers). "What's with this woman?" you are saying about now. "Does she think I have nothing better to do than run around the countryside looking at limestone formations or rebuilt church organs or goofy collections of dressed fleas? Doesn't she know I have more to do with my time than figure out how to spend money on a trip? Why would I want to dig for broken Indian pots or chase around after a bunch of old fogeys who think they're still college kids?"

Well, I'll tell you why: (1) We all live a lot longer than most folks used to, we are up to our ears in labor-saving devices and leisure time after we retire, and unless we discover new interests for ourselves we are of no interest to anyone else. We'll wind up all alone watching "Days of Our Lives" for the rest of our lives. (2) We've played "work-up" ball, taking our turn as it came: going to school, raising a family, making a living or keeping the family going, sending kids to college or the Army or whatever, finally looking after grandkids. Now, before we get any older, it's our turn to go, to cut loose and enjoy whatever appealed to us during those days when family responsibilities and expenses kept us close to home. That's all.

Example: On Oprah Winfrey's show one day the discussion centered on mothers and grown daughters and the tensions between them. "My mother comes to visit me all the time and tries to tell me how to cook," complained one daughter.

"Well," butted in the mother in question, "She was using the wrong pan to cook spaghetti. I always use a bigger pan, I just tried to help her."

"I've been cooking spaghetti in my own pans for fifteen years. I know what pan to use." And the shouting match started again.

Advice from the audience and from some so-called expert was sappy. Do it like Mom says, she's just trying to be helpful.

Now think about this. If that mother had sense enough to go someplace besides her daughter's house "all the time," expecting her daughter to be her entertainment, she'd have more to talk about, more to share with her family than the size of the spaghetti pot. If she rushes in once in a while telling the grandchildren about the dressed fleas in a museum or the fine display of quilts she discovered in the next county, the entire family will be better off.

That's what I mean about purpose of travel. Expanding our horizons is contagious. Next time the mother finds time to visit that daughter, the daughter might say, "Mom, let me show you what we have in our town." And forget the spaghetti.

Whether we shuffle off to Buffalo or ride a burro into the Grand Canyon, opt for exotic tropical beaches or choose to explore the banks of Old Man River, there's a bigger world waiting for us, and it's easier to get to every day. If what I have shared here makes travel more accessible, more pleasant for you, I shall be forever grateful. Now get out there and have a fine time. Send me a card; I'd love hearing from you.

BIBLIOGRAPHY

Bach, Ira, and Susan Wolfson. *Chicago on Foot: Walking Tours of Chicago's Architecture.* Fourth edition. Chicago: Chicago Review Press, 1986.

Chester, Carol. *Going Alone: The Woman's Guide to Travel Know How.* New York: Hippocrene Books, 1987.

Foulke, Robert, and Patricia Foulke. *Daytrips, Getaway Weekends and Budget Vacations in New England.* Second edition. Chester, Conn.: Globe Pequot Press, 1988.

Foulke, Robert, and Patricia Foulke. *Daytrips, Getaway Weekends and Budget Vacations in Mid-Atlantic States.* Chester, Conn.: Globe Pequot Press, 1986.

Frommer's Bed and Breakfast, North America. Special Interest Guide Series. Englewood Cliffs, N.J.: Prentice-Hall, 1985.

Marling, William E., and Clare F. Marling. *The Marling Menu-Master for France.* Marling, 1971.

Murphy, Michael, and Laura Murphy. *Ferryliner Vacations in North America: Ocean Travel and Inland Cruising.* New York: E. P. Dutton, 1988.

Pomada, Elizabeth. *Places to Go with Children in Northern California: More Than 350 Attractions throughout Northern California to Delight Children and Parents*. San Francisco, Calif.: Chronicle Books, 1985.

Reader's Digest Editors. *Off the Beaten Path: A Guide to More Than 1,000 Scenic and Interesting Places Still Uncrowded and Inviting*. New York: Reader's Digest Books, 1987.

Stein, Shifra. *Day Trips: Gas Saving Getaways Less Than Two Hours Away from Greater Kansas City*. Revised edition. S. Stein Products, 1984.

Webster, Harriet. *Favorite Short Trips in New York State*. Yankee Magazine Guidebook Series. Dublin, N.H.: Yankee Books.

Woodson, Jr., LeRoy. *Roadside Food: Good Home-Style Cooking across America*. New York: Stewart, Tabori and Chang, 1986.

Wright, Sarah Bird. *Ferries of America: A Guide to Adventurous Travel*. Atlanta, Ga.: Peachtree Publishers, 1987.

Young, Judith. *Celebrations: America's Best Festivals, Carnivals and Parades*. San Bernardino, Calif.: Borgo Press, 1988.